LOVE BLUE
AMANDA'S STORY

GWYN THORN

DISCLAIMER

This is a work of nonfiction. No names have been changed, no characters invented. It is my memories of the life I shared with my granddaughter, which may be different from others. The information regarding the trial was taken from articles that appeared in the Buckhannon newspaper *The Record Delta* during that time.

The story is interspersed with my memories of conversations I had with others and my interpretation of those events.

The product names used in this book are for identification purposes only. All trademarks and registered trademarks are the property of their respective owners. Other company, product, and service names may be trademarks or service marks of others.

For Amanda

*Thank you for teaching so
many the value of life and the
power of a smile.*

Foreword

Every single day in America, there are police officers, social workers, paramedics, nurses, doctors, and prosecuting attorneys who shoulder their responsibilities of caring for victims of crime. Most with experience will affirm that worst among all criminal cases is child abuse—the seldom discussed and unmatched scourge on society. Those at every level of care for child abuse victims serve in their roles as best they are able, ever mindful of the gory details of savage brutality upon the innocent and defenseless forever etched into their consciousness. "Normal" people are at once shocked and enraged, but they just don't have to deal with the ugly underbelly of society nor the consequences, the specifics of which rightly never make polite dinner table or cocktail party conversation for the rest of us.

My role in this story was as Prosecuting Attorney in Upshur County, West Virginia who twice tried the case for Amanda. Given what was perceived by virtually all in attendance as substantial and undeniable direct physical evidence and persuasive circumstantial evidence.

Some things, however, cannot be forgotten, but life moved on after the trial. And for Amanda, she was blessed with finding a new home.

Parenthood done well is the enormous and daunting undertaking accomplished every day. Were that not fact, organized society would cease to exist. Adoptive parenting carries additional layers of challenge and reward. Parenting of special needs children operate in another universe most might imagine, but never fully comprehend.

If you would make the mistake of simply perceiving *Love Blue, Amanda's Story* as the musing of a highly perceptive and doting "Granny," you would miss many messages and the lessons of Amanda's life: a true story of parenting at its very worst and very best; the reality and horror of child abuse; a precious child robbed of the life she was supposed to enjoy; and the existence of divine intervention providing a life as near normal as possible. It is the profoundly heartwarming saga of a young couple who stepped up "to do the right thing" for the right reasons, guided by their faith and supported by their biological families and their extended community families in West Virginia, Louisiana, and Texas; a window into the reality of the myriad of challenges in dealing with both public perceptions and natural instinctive reactions about the handicapped and challenged among us; accepting people for who they are; the example of loving without exception; the value of life and the power of a smile. I accept that the above summary is a daunting list, but much like the old advertisement for Prego spaghetti sauce, I make this promise: "It's in there!"

I thank the author for the opportunity to achieve some personal closure through penning this foreword and for knowing the rest of the story. I am honored and humbled.

My task would be incomplete and I would be remiss if I failed to acknowledge my profound sense of respect for the magnitude of a lifetime of selflessness displayed by Jennifer and Paul Withey together with the extended Withey clan for their collective example of stepping up and doing the right thing. God Bless them all.

William C. Thurman, Esq.
Buckhannon, WV
2019

Table of Contents

Love Blue – Amanda's Story
Prologue

Some call it fate. Some call it predestination. Others say it is God's will. But whatever it was, a chain of events brought Amanda into our lives. And with that chain, the opportunity to share the story of one of the most remarkable people I would ever know came with her.

The idea of sharing the saga of this beautiful girl's life was years in the making in my head. However, it was one of those ideas that was more like a scene flickering across a screen, no real substance and barely in focus.

With each passing year, it was becoming more and more apparent to me that the world needed to hear Amanda's story and how her existence changed so many lives.

One of the biggest obstacles I would face would be getting permission from her parents, Jennifer and Paul, to write it. They had been hypervigilant in protecting her from the story that brought her into our family, but at the same time, they were extremely cognizant of the effect she had on everyone who met her. My hints of taking on the task were always met with some resistance.

Every generation has an event that is indelibly engrained in memory. Depending on your age, it could be the bombing of Pearl Harbor, little John-John saluting his father's casket as it rolled down Pennsylvania Avenue, or the destruction of the New York Twin Towers.

For me, it was the day I got permission to tell Amanda's story. I was at lunch with Jennifer, taking a break from Christmas shopping in 2015. I don't recall how or why the subject came up. Maybe it was my stubborn streak or the fact that I don't like being told I can't do something. But as we were enjoying PF Chang's Lettuce Wraps and sharing an order of Mongolian Beef, something told me to ask again.

Jennifer and I have completely different memories of the conversation. What I heard, with the same exasperation that had been in her voice when I used to tell her to clean her room, was, "Yes, Mom, you can write Amanda's story." Jennifer's recollection of the conversation was her saying, "Mom, I can't stop you." Apparently, we hear what we want to hear.

I was ecstatic. Shopping was now secondary in my thoughts. All I wanted to do was get to Jennifer's house and share the big news.

As we walked into the living room, Amanda was surrounded by the color red. She was sitting in her red wheelchair. Her respite worker, Shante, had braided her hair and placed a red flower over her right ear. She was wearing a red t-shirt that was dotted with snowflakes and her nails had been painted to match the flower.

The smile on her face confirmed what we all knew. Christmas was her favorite time of year. She was ready for the festivities of the holiday to begin.

"Hello, my beautiful Amanda," I said as I leaned down and gave her a hug. Sometimes I think she had a knack for reading minds, because the sparkle in her blue eyes was illuminating the room more than the lights on the tree. As is true with people who are blind or deaf, different senses are heightened to accommodate the loss. There were times when I even wondered if she was psychic. She seemed to sense when big news was about to be announced.

Maybe she had the ability to read people's faces to make up for her inability to communicate verbally. Or, maybe it was the smile on my face that clued her into what she was about to hear. Regardless, her eyes never failed to communicate her every thought.

There had been a look of knowing on her face as I walked in the door. She knew something was up and had picked up on my excitement. I had seen that same smile on her face when her aunt Cia asked her to be the flower girl in her wedding. And again when Becca, a family friend for twenty plus years, and Mark, Paul's brother, got engaged. When they told her the news, she was thrilled, but when they asked if she would be in the wedding, her smile reflected the excitement in her eyes.

It's hard to articulate how exceptional her smile was. There were subtle nuances that I had come to know. Right side turned up when she watched her siblings do something silly. Left side turned up when she was deep in thought about what was going on around her. Right side turned downward when she was annoyed with someone interrupting her favorite show. Left side turned down when she had her fill of watching football—unless it was the Steelers playing.

It was rare for her to not have at least a partial smile gracing her face. But when Amanda was truly excited about something, both corners of her mouth would turn up and her dimples became even more pronounced. Over the years, we all got very good at reading that smile. Her eyes and her smile were her tools for communicating, and she used them to let us know she was fully aware and comprehended everything that was going on around her.

The imaginary talks with her started when we first met. My mind had always wondered what her voice would sound like if we were talking. Would it be soft and mellow? Deep and throaty? Or a sweet tone with a hint of shyness?

It may seem strange, but from the first time I held her in my arms, I had pretend conversations with her. We talked about everything from the weather to the headlines of the day, the cute boy she had her eye on, or the latest baseball game her brothers or sister had played. I knew she couldn't respond with words, but the expression on her face told me what she was thinking. This time was no different.

As I continued to hug her, I whispered, "You are not going to believe what your Mom and I talked about at lunch." Her eyes were studying my face. She knew something big was coming.

"She said I could write your story and tell the world how special you are."

"Seriously, Mom said you could write my story?! I wonder what made her finally give in," were the words I heard.

"I don't know, Manda Panda" I said, using the nickname I called her. "Maybe she realized that it is hard for people to understand the value of life when the persona that the world sees doesn't conform to the norm. Maybe she realized how important it is for others to know the good you have done without ever speaking a word. Regardless of her reason, I'm so thankful that she said I could."

"Oh my gosh! I can't believe it. But are you sure you want to take this on? It's not going to be easy. I'll understand if you decide you can't or don't want to do it."

In my mind, her voice was cracking with a hint of sadness. Part of me felt that she might be worried that I really wouldn't write it. She knew parts of the story would make people sad and cause others to feel sorry for her. But her hope was that most would read it and appreciate how precious her life was to her, regardless of her limitations.

For me, now that I had permission to tell her story, the reality of what was at stake started to sink in. There was a knot forming in the pit of my stomach, and for a moment, I was questioning my sanity. Telling her I was going to write her story was the equivalent of opening Pandora's box. There would be no turning back.

Sharing her story was one thing, but giving her the voice she never had wouldn't be easy. I knew I had to find a way to let others know that what they saw as a broken shell was instead a spirit that longed to soar. I would give this beautiful soul who dreamed of sharing the most personal details of her life the means to let the world know what she had accomplished without her ever saying a word.

As I sat there and held her hand, there was still a part of me that screamed, "What the heck are you thinking? You can't do this." But as the smile on her face continued to light up the room with happiness, I knew I couldn't let her down.

That no matter what it took, I would chronicle the years of this remarkable young woman and share the journey that was her life. Her eyes told me that she believed in me. They told me she trusted me with the two things she had always longed for. That she could finally have the conversations she dreamed of having. And more importantly, that the world would know the value of her life.

Chapter 1

Many could argue as to what triggered Amanda becoming a part of our crazy family. It most likely started with Jennifer working with the special needs program in high school. She had opted out of the regular PE class to assist with the special needs kids during their physical activity hour.

She was one of those people who was often referred to as an old soul. Her level of kindness and desire to do the right thing was not often seen in a teenager. But her affinity for those with disabilities started with her exposure to the programs at Plano East High School. And that experience would guide her during her college years. It is what gave me an even deeper appreciation of a heart brimming with more compassion and empathy than I had ever seen before.

When she left for college at the tender age of sixteen, I was terrified of what lay ahead of her. She was way too young to be on her own, but we can't keep those we love from moving forward with their lives.

It was the summer after her freshman year at Texas Christian University that she met Paul, a PhD candidate in the physics department. His Canadian mother had warned him, "Be careful around those girls in Texas. You know they get married really young down there."

At that first meeting, Paul refused to believe she was seventeen and asked to see her driver's license. Instead of running away as fast as he could, he fell in love even faster as they spent hours talking about their individual goals for the future. And she fell in love just as quickly. As our family got to know him, it was easy to see he was a kind and caring young man whose heart was as big and full of love for others as it was for Jennifer.

• • •

They married two years after that first meeting and then finished up their respective degrees. Now all that lay ahead of them was to start their careers, raise a family, and live happily ever after.

It didn't take much for Paul to land a job in the quaint little town of Buckhannon, West Virginia located in the foothills of the Allegheny Mountains after graduation. He would be teaching subjects – physics and astronomy – that he loved and Jennifer would start the process of setting up their home. It was easy to see this dynamic duo was well on their way to building a life filled with joy, laughter, and love.

West Virginia Wesleyan was the quintessential small-town college campus with Georgian style architecture of red brick buildings with white steeples that were built in the early 1900's and later mixed with the modern architectural designs incorporated in the mid 80's. There were tree-lined sidewalks of sprouting white oaks, red pines, and sweet gums interspersed with spacious outdoor common areas. In spring and summer, those areas were filled with young students sitting on blankets and studying. Fall would find those same scholars nestled among the multi-colored leaves that signaled the soon-to-be snow covered grounds.

But in the fall of 1994, the beauty and tranquility of what many categorized as the picture-perfect postcard rural city would be shaken to its core. The day the story broke, the headlines read "Man Accused of Severely Beating Girl." One could envision the collective gasp as the residents woke to the news. How the air was sucked out of the city as they realized 'the girl' was a three-year-old baby.

• • •

What led Amanda to our doorstep was a Wednesday night prayer meeting a few days after Christmas in 1994. During the service, members of the congregation could make a prayer request. Normally family members are asking for prayers for a loved one who is sick, or maybe a sibling dealing with personal issues or other life challenges.

That night, there was one appeal for support that was different from others that were normally made. This one was on behalf of a local social worker. She was desperately looking for a home for the little girl who had been making headlines in the local newspaper for the past two months.

Finding a home is hard enough when a child can function. Placement is even more difficult for a child with learning disabilities or behavioral issues. But for any Child Protective Services (CPS) worker, finding a home for a little girl who would be completely dependent for all her needs was the equivalent of climbing Kilimanjaro. Besides the normal things such as brushing teeth or hair, this soon to be four-year-old would be in diapers for the rest of her life. She would need to be tube fed multiple times a day and would be coming with a list of instructions and medications that took up several 8x10 sheets of paper.

She would never be able to tell her foster parents if she had a stomachache, was thirsty, felt hot or cold, or what doll she wanted to play with. The social worker in charge of her case, Paula Hinzman, knew that the hardest part for any foster parent, however, would be the blank, emotionless stare that filled Amanda's face.

What happened that night in the prayer service would be the first of many miracles that would grace our lives. Jennifer and Paul left the church and prayed for a sign. They discussed the pros and cons. They questioned whether they were ready, but ultimately left it in God's hands to show them a sign.

As is the case in most situations, God doesn't take out a billboard telling us what to do. Instead, He opens our hearts and lets us know we are going in the right direction. The next morning, they had a partial answer. They would make the ninety-minute drive to the rehab facility where Amanda was being cared for to meet her.

Not long after I started writing Amanda's story, Jennifer and I talked about that first meeting. I was desperately trying to fill in the gaps of my memory and hoping to shed new light on Amanda's journey to our family.

"Um...what do I remember most about that first meeting with Amanda?" said Jennifer. "That's a difficult question. But there are a few things that still stand out in my mind. One was the conversation, actually it was a lecture, from the doctor. Her professional demeanor was reinforced with the starched white coat and the matter-of-fact way she told us about Amanda's condition.

"She did her best to give the appearance of being the hard-nosed by-the-book doctor. Her stethoscope hung around her neck, but the light brown shoulder length hair gave her a softness that said she cared about her patients. But the level of detachment she tried to keep was completely gone when it came to Amanda. It was easy to see that she was one of her all-time favorites. Maybe it was because of the fighting spirit she saw in Amanda. Or maybe she saw Amanda's future and knew how she would change others. Regardless, when she stroked Amanda's arm while she filled us in on her needs, it was easy to see how deeply she cared for her."

Jennifer's mood turned somber as she continued reminiscing. "However, I think Paula was wondering if the doctor was trying to sabotage the placement at the beginning of our meeting with her. She was going through the litany of instructions and detailing the medication that would need to be administered on a daily basis. We all knew she was just doing her due diligence, but for a few minutes, there was a part of me that wondered if we were up for the challenge. It was after that first meeting that I called and talked to you about Amanda.

"I know we were in the process of being certified as foster parents, but I was only twenty-two years old. I think that was a fact that may have been overlooked or somehow wasn't noticed."

The serious expression on her face suddenly changed. I could tell she was remembering something from that first meeting that made her smile. "I remember looking at Amanda in the bed. All of the tubes that had sustained her life were gone by the time we met her.

"She had a button in her stomach that was used for feeding, and from what Paula had told us, most of her hair was now growing back. I wasn't sure what the next step was, but then Paul looked at Paula and asked if he could hold Amanda."

The look of love for her husband that I had seen so many times cross her face was magnified with that memory. "Whenever we see an infant, the first thing most of us do is ask if we can hold the baby. But Amanda was an average size and weight for an almost four-year-old. It would be the first time of many that I would see her sitting on his lap."

She paused and took a minute to enjoy the scene that was playing over in her mind from that first meeting. "Mom, I so wish we had cell phones back then the way we do now. I would have cherished capturing that moment. It was something I would see him do so many times over the years. I think he was a little sad when she was no longer small enough to fit in his lap."

It was obvious that the memories were taking their emotional toll, but she finally continued with the story. "But as she grew, his routine changed with her. He was always happy to have her sitting next to him on the couch. So many times, I would look up from whatever I was doing and see one or more of the kids in his lap.

"They would be reading books together, watching the latest favorite Disney show, or he would be teaching them about hockey as they watched a playoff game. As our brood grew, sometimes I couldn't see him for all of the kids."

She laughed out loud and smiled remembering those days. I nodded in understanding. Jennifer was the heart of the family, but Paul was the glue that kept them all together.

"Mom, I really wondered that day what we were getting ourselves into, but in my heart, I knew we were doing the right thing."

I thought her story was over until I saw the tears form in her eyes. "The one thing that overwhelmed me when Paul and I first walked into her room were the framed pictures of Amanda that adorned every counter as well as ten or more stuffed animals surrounding her in her bed. There were pictures of her and her mom. There were pictures of her with her grandparents. Pictures of her with friends and cousins. But the one that brought tears to my eyes was the 3x5 portrait picture that was taken when she had just turned three."

As it was with many of the memories about those early days, they often were associated with moments of sadness as well. She was holding back the tears, but continued telling me the story. "When we went back a few days later to get her, all of the pictures were gone except that one lone portrait as well as only one stuffed animal in her bed. Her biological family had taken all remnants and reminders of her life with them."

Her head dropped in sadness. "It appeared that they didn't want her to have any memories of them in her new life. That is everyone except her 'Pappy.' He is the only one who reached out to me and asked if he could see Amanda. I took her every time he called, but eventually, I think it just became too painful for him. The irony is that he wasn't biologically related to her, but he was the only one who asked to see her."

I have no doubt that as they were driving away from the rehab center, Jennifer and Paul knew they were up for the challenge of giving Amanda a new life. The tragedy that brought her into our family was never going to change. Her life as she knew it was over, but a whole new life was starting for her.

What none of us realized was that with that tragedy, the lives of our family and so many others would be transformed forever.

Chapter 2

Because they never felt it was pertinent to the situation, Jennifer and Paul rarely told anyone what happened to Amanda. To tell how she went from being the normal healthy little girl who is pictured on the cover of this book holding her friend's doll, to the little girl who could no longer speak, feed herself, control her arms or legs, or have dreams the same as others, is not an easy story to tell.

It would be much simpler to process emotionally if I said she had been in a horrific car wreck or fell off a swing set and broke her back. But that's not what happened. And according to the trial that followed, there are still many unanswered questions.

All that anyone knows is that in the fall of 1994, Amanda went to bed a normal, healthy little girl. And somewhere between 10 pm and 7 am, something happened that left her with a medical diagnosis comparable to what doctors often term as a persistent vegetative state.

Some may not understand why I didn't know the details of what happened until I started writing this book. If truth be told, my mind had been comfortable telling myself that she probably started crying, and the person who was taking care of Amanda that night snapped. Maybe the cries for her mom were too much to handle. Maybe a drunken stupor caused the perpetrator to get annoyed when she couldn't be comforted. Or possibly, that in a state of being high on drugs, a pillow was used to try and drown out the noise by covering her face.

Something inside of me had felt there was more to the story, but by not knowing the facts, I could believe whatever I wanted.

The one part of the book I wasn't looking forward to writing was the story of the trial. My normally analytical mind hadn't worked through the specifics of how to approach the subject.

I thought back to when I told Amanda I was going to write her memoir. The outline of the book was years in the making in my head and eventually found its way to paper. But while the majority of ideas were written down, the part about the trial was a mystery. My notes simply stated *call the prosecuting attorney who handled the case, find out details, read the transcript from the trial.*

It took me months, but I finally dug deep enough for the courage to make the call that I had been dreading. As I dialed the number, I wasn't sure what I was going to say or how I would start the conversation. My heart was beating double-time as I listened to the phone ring. For a brief instant, I contemplated hanging up. But then the voice on the other end answered, and I knew I had to push forward and get the details as best I could.

"Hello, this is Bill Thurman. How can I help you?"

"Hi, Mr. Thurman. My name is Gwyn Thorn. I'm Amanda Withey's grandmother. I know you probably don't remember me, but we met when you handled Amanda's adoption for my daughter and son-in-law."

"Actually, I do recall that day quite vividly. It was a privilege to be a part of the proceedings. Kind of helped me get some peace."

His words were muffled by the cracking of his voice. It's as if he knew the questions I was about to ask and though it pained him to relive what he later told me was the 'single worst case he ever had to try as a lawyer,' he was still willing to talk to me.

I knew that Amanda's trial was challenging for him. But I knew it was vital to the story itself. My heart sank, knowing I was going to be dredging up memories that he hoped would eventually leave his brain.

"Mr. Thurman, the reason I wanted to talk to you was that several months ago, I told Amanda that I was going to write her life story. I know the trial is not the part that Jennifer wants me to tell, but I can't do her life justice without including some information about what happened to her and the trial that followed."

My mind saw the image of the tall, dark headed lawyer who had stood in the parking lot of the local diner with me after the adoption proceedings. I remember thinking how formidable he must have been in those early years of his career. But my heart still breaks as I remember the tear that rolled down his cheek when he told me that it was the one case that would forever haunt him.

The lump in his throat made the words almost impossible to say, but he pressed on. "It's been over twenty years, but just thinking about this brings tears to my eyes" were the first words he said. "You can't imagine what it is like to have to present that kind of evidence to a jury. The testimony of all the doctors, nurses, Child Protective Advocates, and witnesses spoke for itself.

"But the hardest part was entering photographs into evidence. They detailed over sixty bruises, burns, bites, and choke marks. The memory of them still shakes me to my core."

My heart constricted in my chest; the tears started rolling down my face. I prayed that God would give me the courage to go on, but I felt as if I had just been hit by a runaway freight train. I was doing my best to hold back the floodgate of tears that were minutes from erupting.

In some ways, I was ashamed that I had never asked for details, but I was so relieved that I hadn't known until now. Part of me believes that by not knowing, I could love her without being overwhelmed with a different level of sadness that would have accompanied the vision of her battered and almost lifeless body that was brought to the emergency room at St. Joseph's the day of the 'incident.'

Luckily, before I could say anything, he continued, "That beautiful baby had been brutalized. I can't even comprehend how evil and wicked a person would have to be to do what was done to her. She wasn't even four years old. God knows I've tried to come to grips with what happened more times than I can remember."

He paused, and I was left speechless. It was obvious even without seeing his face that he was struggling with telling me more and sharing his memories. "All I know is there is a special place in hell for the person who did this to her."

My heart broke for this man I had met only once in my life. Nothing would ever ease the pain of having to prosecute a trial of this nature. Nothing would ever give Amanda back the life that was stolen from her.

I would come to learn the entire story as I researched the trial. I would have the opportunity to meet with people who were instrumental in gathering evidence for the case. I would talk to some of the locals who knew her when she was little.

What stood out the most from those conversations was seeing how the memory of what happened to Amanda still affected those that I spoke with even after twenty years. There was guilt over wondering if the signs of possible abuse were missed or ignored. There was the second guessing of 'would things have been different if Amanda had been invited to a sleep over to give her mom a break?' But there were also grins as they talked about her sparkling blue eyes, her long curly hair, and the dimples that appeared each time she smiled.

Chapter 3

There are certain ways you imagine your first child or grandchild coming into your life, but the thought of my daughter sitting day after day in a courtroom is not what I ever envisioned. Instead, I saw Jennifer reliving all of the firsts that I marveled over when she was little. The first words, the first steps, the first day of school, the first crush.

You are filled with sorrow as you realize that your child will have to struggle through illnesses, broken bones, mean kids at school, and their first heartbreak. Knowing all the while that every moment, both good and bad, adds flavor to each of our lives.

As I contemplated how to tell Amanda's story, one of the first things that came to mind was that we knew nothing about the first few years of her life. Unfortunately, my mind can only speculate on her life in those years before we were blessed to have her as a part of our family.

One part of me wants to believe that when Amanda was born, her biological mother was overcome with happiness as she held her baby girl for the first time. How she carefully unwrapped the blanket that was swaddling her so that she could count her fingers and toes. How she must have been awed by the sweet cry of her newborn.

I want to believe that she was filled with the same anticipation and anxiety that so many experience when they become first time parents. That she struggled with the same fears we all have as we take on this new role. And that each time she introduced Amanda to a grandparent, aunt, uncle, cousin, or friend, her heart was filled with pride as they gushed over her precious infant saying how beautiful and perfect she was.

When she chose her name, did she intend to call her Amy, Mandy, or Amanda? Did she dream of her one day becoming a doctor, lawyer, or teacher? Did she see her being a cheerleader in high school or maybe the star pitcher of the softball team? Did she wonder if she was going to be tall and stately with long, straight blond hair, or maybe small and petite with curly auburn locks? Was she mesmerized by her beautiful blue eyes?

My mind wanders to visions of Amanda's many firsts and those milestones that mark the passing of time. I see the mischievous little girl who did the normal things that often try a parent's patience. It is easy to imagine her spitting out the peas or dumping the bowl of cheerios on the floor for her puppy to scoop up. I imagine the delight on her parents' faces the first time she said 'Mama' or 'Dada.'

I can't imagine what Amanda's biological mom might have thought if she knew that the precious gift she was given would one day be robbed of the life she dreamed for her. Would she have broken down and wept uncontrollably for hours? Would she have done more to protect her? Would she have made the choice to abort the pregnancy if she knew what was awaiting Amanda?

The protective side of me was filled with concern as I thought of Jennifer taking on the role of becoming Amanda's mother. Knowing that she was never going to see her daughter do those things. Not knowing the depth of sacrifice and hardship that lay ahead for her family as they embark on the journey of taking care of a person with so many limitations and needs.

Simultaneously, my heart was bursting with pride knowing the level of selflessness that is required to take on the role. I knew if anyone could rise to the challenge, it would be Jennifer and Paul. I knew they would do everything they could to ensure that despite the obstacles; Amanda would have a full life. They would make sure that even though her life seemed worthless to others, it would never be worthless to them or to Amanda.

They were graced with knowing without really knowing, that this beautiful little girl would be able to change the lives of those around her as well as hundreds, if not thousands, of others.

Chapter 4

The trial had not begun when I first met Amanda in the spring of 1995 as this newly formed family made the trek from West Virginia to Houston, Dallas, and Baton Rouge to meet her new family that would consist of grandparents, great-grandparents, great-great-grandparents, aunts, and uncles. Nothing was mentioned about the upcoming trial or any details they might have been privy to. They were focused on giving Amanda a life that was as normal as possible. To them, the story of what happened to Amanda was not pertinent as to how anyone **would** or **should** treat her.

Even though Jennifer and I had talked many times on the phone, I had no idea what to expect with that first meeting. All I know is that my heart melted as soon as I saw her. The curls wrapped softly around her face, and she seemed tiny for a four-year-old. Her arms were bent at the elbow, but they were stiff, and the movements she made were strained. The edge of the right side of her mouth was slightly turned up with the softest hint of dimple. But what struck me more than anything were the beautiful blue eyes that followed my every move.

It's hard to understand, but in that moment, I wasn't seeing a broken child, but a beautiful little girl who was perfect in every way. And I was witnessing the bond that Jennifer and Paul had with her.

As I moved closer, I was momentarily lost as to how I should treat her. If she were a newborn, it would have been easy. I could have cradled her in my arms and gently stroked the top of her head. I could have uncurled her fingers and been in awe when they clasped around my finger. But I had no idea what would be the right thing to say or do with this little girl.

"Mom, she isn't made out of glass," Jennifer said when she saw my hesitation. "I know. But is there anything I should know or be aware of? I don't want to hurt her." Being around someone with so many issues was just not something I was familiar with, and I was terrified of doing something that could hurt her.

I don't think my daughter had ever seen me afraid. I had been the strong single mom for most of her life. In many ways, I was invincible in her eyes. But when it came to Amanda, she knew this was uncharted territory for me. She smiled and gave me a quick hug. "Don't worry about doing anything wrong. Paul and I have made a promise to her that we are going to treat her the way we would any child. And with what she has been through, it's fairly obvious that she is stronger than anyone I've ever known.

"You may not remember, but when she was in the hospital after the 'incident,' a Do Not Resuscitate order was in place. She fought back on her own twice. She has a purpose in life, and we intend to see that she has every opportunity to show the world why she is still here." She then added with a laugh, "I promise, you can't break her."

As she placed Amanda on my lap, I gently wrapped my arm around her. I wondered if she would understand my words. If she would be comforted knowing that she had a completely new family that was going to love her. As our eyes met for the first time, she gave me that signature smile that would light up my world over and over again.

"Hi Amanda. I'm your new granny. I think we are going to be very good friends." As I leaned closer and gave her an Eskimo kiss, the light from within came shining through. Little did I know that I was about to have my first imaginary conversation with her.

"Hi Granny. You look funny when you wrinkle your nose," she said, giggling.

"You mean when I do this?" rubbing my nose back and forth across hers again.

"That tickles. But it's kind of cool. Are you always going to be sooo silly?" was the question I heard.

"I think it's my job to make you laugh. But know I'm here to listen if you want to talk."

"That would be nice. I'm still trying to figure it all out. I can't do many of the things I used to do. And I'm a little confused about what happened to my old mommy, but I really am very happy to have my new mommy and daddy. Do you think I will ever see my other mommy again?" she asked.

"That's not the way this works, sweetheart. Sometimes things happen and you have to have a new mommy and daddy."

That thought seemed to bring a look of sadness to Amanda's face sparking a tug at my heart that I had never experienced before. I wasn't sure if it was the love that filled my heart when I first saw her, or the sadness of knowing that the life that she was supposed to have was no longer a part of her reality.

But as I held her, I knew there was something unique about this little girl named Amanda. That she was going to have a huge impact not only on my life, but on so many others. And I think in some way she knew it as well.

Chapter 5

As Jennifer and Paul headed back to West Virginia, they were not only faced with what was now their 'new norm,', but of a trial that was looming on the horizon.

I thought of how the scenarios that play out in our minds are rarely the same as reality. As I watched Jennifer and her younger sister, Marcia (pronounced Mar-See-Uh), grow and mature into the beautiful young women they became, I pictured them having the perfect life that I didn't have.

Reality, however, presents itself in a myriad of ways. As much as we wish we could keep our children from ever experiencing anything negative, nothing keeps them from dealing with their own challenges. All we can do is hope that we prepare them as much as possible for what comes their way.

For Jennifer and Paul, taking on the responsibility of Amanda was more than the day-to-day obligations. Not only was there the joy of the beautiful little girl who was now a part of their lives, but there was the reality of the impending trial. They would be making the trek to the neighboring county to sit through the proceedings that would mesmerize two different counties in rural West Virginia.

The details of the trial are not what I want anyone to focus on as I share the story of Amanda's life. But it is important to understand how she went from being a fully functioning child to one with no chance of ever recovering from her injuries and having what most people think of as a normal life.

Because I knew so little about the actual trial itself, I knew I had to do research to get the details. My first thought was to try and get a copy of the transcript from the proceedings. Unfortunately, the trial notes, pictures, and other pertinent pieces of information had been archived twenty years earlier. Although it might have been possible to force the state to produce the records, I think the truth is that it was just too painful for many to dredge up those memories.

The prosecuting attorney, social worker, and "cub" reporter who wrote most of the articles that were used to fill in the details of the trial were all willing to talk to me. And at the same time, it tested their emotions. The memories that had long been buried were still extremely painful even after twenty years.

As I look back on it, I'm glad that I wasn't able to see the pictures that were part of the evidence used in the trial. My mind didn't need or want to be bombarded with the images of the girl I love so much with bruises, bite marks, and burns covering most of her tiny body.

From the account in the newspaper, many of the members of the jury couldn't handle these images either. Some looked away. Others had tears in their eyes as they were shown the pictures that were taken by the social worker within hours of Amanda being brought into the emergency room.

• • •

The following is a recap of the articles that were in the small town's thrice-weekly newspapers interspersed with conversations I had with those directly involved in the case. The best I can do is lay out the evidence as it was presented through those articles as it was told to the jury.

As often happens with a case that has been the main headline in news, TV, and radio, the first motion put forth by the defense attorney was to seek a change of venue. Can't blame him, as I'm certain there wasn't a single adult in the town of 6,200 people who hadn't either seen the headlines or had a conversation with a friend or neighbor about what had happened. Although I'm not sure what difference a distance of fifteen miles was going to make in the jury pool, the trial was moved from Upshur County to Lewis County.

Not only was there a change in venue, but before the trial started, the judge told Jennifer that she could not bring Amanda to the proceedings. If his aim had been to protect her because she was a minor, I could somewhat understand his reasoning. But his explanation to Jennifer was that seeing Amanda could prejudice the jury against the defendant.

Part of me wants to go into a diatribe about how Amanda deserved to be part of the proceedings. Maybe I've watched too many episodes of *Law and Order*, but I can't fathom how a plaintiff can be barred from a courtroom when they are the victim. It is one thing hearing from CPS that a normal healthy little girl is now in a vegetative state and will never have control of her extremities, be able to talk or take care of herself, but it is another thing to see her in person.

As I read accounts of the testimony, I realized that in my initial conversation with Bill, he had graciously held back the details. Maybe he thought I already knew the complete story. Or maybe he sensed that I wasn't fully aware of the extent of her injuries, and he didn't want to be the person who told me. What I was certain of was that the memories still haunted him, and no amount of time was ever going to erase seeing the battered body of Amanda that fateful morning in October of 1994.

As the transcript from the trial was not available, my best guess as to the opening remarks from Mr. Thurman would probably have been something similar to the following:

"Ladies and gentlemen of the jury, this isn't going to be an easy trial. The injuries sustained by this three-and-a-half year old little girl include bruises all over her face, head, and shoulders. We will show you pictures of multiple burns on her torso, legs, and back that are consistent with someone holding a curling iron against her flesh, as well as multiple bite marks on her body.

"And ladies and gentlemen, along with the physical abuse sustained by this innocent child, you will hear about four counts of sexual assault."

It's easy to imagine that every person listening to the proceedings must have stifled the desire to run out of the courtroom and literally throw up. Never far from anyone's thoughts was the knowledge that the victim was a toddler.

The defense attorney, however, presented a completely different picture in his opening statement. He maintained that his client was asleep and had no idea how Amanda was injured and shifted the blame to another possible suspect.

According to the newspaper article, he opened by telling the jury, "but there is at least one other person who had opportunity, motive, and means, and this person did do it." He was referring to the defendant's ex-wife.

The first witness for the prosecution was the county sheriff. Law enforcement officials are often seen as tough and rugged individuals, but his testimony was filled with emotion as he described the condition of the three-year-old he saw in the hospital that morning in October. He told of the multiple bruises on her head, shoulders, and chest area as the sixteen photos taken by Child Protective Services were placed into evidence.

The sheriff testified that he had conversations with both the defendant and Amanda's biological mother. They both agreed to voluntary blood and urine samples, dental impressions and a search of the residence where the attack allegedly took place. He recounted how he, along with another deputy and the social worker, Paula Hinzman, searched the residence and found no evidence of forced entry into the home. Those facts, along with the defendant's voluntary remarks about having bit Amanda two weeks earlier, were enough for him to arrest the defendant and for the Prosecuting Attorney to eventually bring charges.

On cross-examination, the defense attorney pressed the witness about the evidentiary value of much of the evidence taken from the house. According to the accounts, the majority of the evidence removed from the premises had no bearing on the case. He was also able to get the sheriff to say that there was no proof—meaning there was no semen—to make a conclusive statement that the alleged sexual attacks were committed by a male. He was alluding to the idea and hoping the jury would believe that an object created the sexual trauma. Needless to say, the defense attorney was doing his best to poke holes into the evidence as it was presented.

If I were to title this chapter, it would be *Why I Hate Jury Duty*. Trials are not always about presenting the truth, but planting that seed of doubt in the minds of the jury. It is for that very reason that I have an aversion to participating in our legal process. That self-doubt is often without reason or merit. Words are often twisted and excuses made that most reasonable and sane people will ignore, but that isn't always the case.

The second witness to take the stand was Paula Hinzman, the social worker assigned to Amanda's case. She produced a photograph of Amanda taken before the assault. She was asked if there were any specific orders in place regarding Amanda. She responded that there were strict instructions stating that the defendant's family was not allowed to visit Amanda. Other directions put in place were specifically for Amanda's biological mother. She was barred from being alone with her and all narcotic drugs were required to be locked when she was in the hospital room.

Next, there was evidence presented from a doctor and LPN who administered the sex crime test, as well as the testimony of the nun in charge of pastoral care at St. Joseph's. The nun recounted her conversation with the defendant and Amanda's biological mother.

She stated that both told her they had no knowledge of the attack. The defendant, however, did ask her if the attack could get him into any trouble. She testified that she thought that was an odd question to ask.

The emergency room director then testified regarding the medical procedures administered by the hospital. He stated that the excess of acid in Amanda's blood was consistent with her having been deprived of oxygen for an extended period of time. It was his expert opinion that she was suffocated or choked.

The prosecution presented additional information supplied by the pediatrician at the hospital Amanda was transferred to when it was evident that St. Joseph's was not equipped to handle her injuries. The doctor stated that she suffered over seventy separate injuries from the attack. In his testimony, he said, "I honestly don't believe there was any part of her body spared from trauma."

Unfortunately, it was part of the pediatrician's notes that the defense used to build their case. His notes chronicled a conversation with Amanda's biological mother where she said she suspected the defendant's ex-wife of coming into the trailer and attacking Amanda. Later evidence from a deputy told a different story. He testified that Amanda's biological mother told him that she believed the defendant was responsible for the attack.

Some of the most damning evidence, however, were the bite marks on Amanda's body. A forensic odonatologist testified that the marks were made by the defendant. The defense tried to get the expert to state that the bites could have occurred the previous day, but he held fast to his statement. "I still hold the opinion, with reasonable scientific certainty, these wounds were made six to eight hours before the photographs were taken."

Before the prosecution rested, a doctor who was a member of the child advocacy team at the second hospital took the stand. She corroborated the testimony regarding the sexual assault and catalogued the various bruises, bites, and burn marks on the body. According to her, "there was no piece of skin on the entire head or scalp that was not bruised or swollen."

She testified that many of the injuries were on top of others. The most severe was a brain injury caused by constriction of the carotid on both sides of Amanda's throat that were consistent with choking. Her final words before cross-examination were, "This was, by far, the worst abuse case I've seen in my career. She was horribly beaten, strangulated, and sexually abused."

The defense attorney again tried to get her to say that there was no way to tell if the sexual injuries were caused by a male sex organ. However, she stood her ground and said the sexual injuries were made by a penis.

After the prosecution rested its case, the main witness for the defense was the defendant himself. Upon taking the stand, he recounted the days leading up to the attack. He told of having returned from a job in a neighboring state and going to his brother's house the following day to watch football. He talked about going back to the trailer later that night where he heard Amanda's biological mother spanking the child while he was in the shower. He said he then fell asleep and never heard anything.

He told the jury that he woke around 7:45 am and found Amanda lying on the floor beside the bathroom. He testified that he picked her up and put her on his bed. He stated that Amanda was semi-conscious when he found her on the floor. He claimed he asked her what was wrong. His testimony was that she replied, "I just don't feel good."

Closing arguments were made and the jury was given instructions on the counts. All that remained in the minds of the prosecution and others who had diligently collected and presented the evidence was how many years the defendant would spend in jail.

Chapter 6

Before I continue, I want to reiterate that my reason for writing this book is to let the world know what a remarkable life Amanda had once she joined our family. How proud she made all of us with the way she inspired others with her smile and the love that poured forth from her eyes. How amazed we all were with her strength and resilience.

The 'incident' that led to the trial was the catalyst for her being a part of our lives. The outcome had no effect on what she went on to accomplish. It had no bearing on 'the rest of the story' as the iconic American broadcaster Paul Harvey used to say.

I can only imagine after reading the previous chapter about the trial that there isn't a single person who doesn't want to know how many years the defendant was sentenced to or better yet, if the death penalty could apply in such a case.

But as I remembered the conversations I had with my dad as a young teenager about the fairness of life, I'm struck with the phrase I hated the most. "Gwynnie, no one ever promised that life was going to be fair."

For me personally, there are several things that strike me as odd about the testimony of the defendant from the accounts that I read in the newspaper articles. One is that he said he could hear her biological mother spanking the girl while he was in the shower, yet he slept through her being brutalized by another person who entered the house without his knowledge.

The second was him saying that when he found Amanda, she told him she didn't feel well. How does someone who is brought into an emergency room with the level of injuries she had, and who was diagnosed as being in a vegetative state have any interaction with the defendant? My mind isn't making the leap from semi-conscious to vegetative state.

And third, there is no way he didn't see the physical injuries on her. No one can say how they would react in any traumatic situation, but I can't imagine how anyone wouldn't have swooped her up, run out of the trailer, and started pounding on doors begging someone to call 911.

Instead, he testified that he waited for her biological mother to arrive. He didn't tell her the extent of the injuries (which validates that he did see them). He went on to clarify that he didn't tell her "for fear she would be upset while driving to his home and possibly have an accident."

• • •

The jury took forty minutes to find the defendant *Not Guilty* on the four counts of sexual assault, but they were hung on the child abuse charges, which led to a second trial.

The outcome of the second trial on the remaining charges several months later was a headline of *Not Guilty*.

There were a lot of rumors and gossip as to how something like that could have happened. I am only stating some of the following as a means of explanation and am in no way saying any of it is true.

As I reflected on what I read from the newspaper, there were several pieces of the puzzle that were missing and questions that needed answers. The first question in my mind had to do with the defendants ex-wife who the defense attorney tried to say had brutalized Amanda. The prosecuting attorney and sheriff both corroborated that she was never a suspect. She was able to account for her whereabouts during the time of the assault.

One fact that I felt was most telling was something Jennifer had mentioned to me at the time of the trial back in 1995. In my talks with Mr. Thurman he attested to the fact that what Jennifer had told me back then was true. The day after the verdict was rendered, he got a call from one of the members of the jury. Maybe it was feelings of guilt or remorse for not having let the judge know what was going on, but she called Mr. Thurman wanting to know if she could change her vote. The conversation detailed how one member of the jury was bullying the others to find the defendant not guilty.

That conversation alone makes the rumors about members from both juries being tampered with an unfortunate possibility. The stories of several jury members suddenly having a new truck, car or boat due to bribes will never be proven. It is strictly hearsay and speculation.

What troubles me most is the reaction – or lack thereof – by the residents of Upshur County. With the ex-wife ruled out as a suspect and the jury believing that the defendant slept through the brutal attack on Amanda, it's hard for me to understand how this town that was equivalent to a modern day Mayberry was not outraged on one hand and terrified on the other?

I would have thought that there would be a near hysterical response to the not guilty verdicts. My personal reaction would have been to double bolt all of my doors and windows for fear that my little one might be the next victim. I would have been concerned that a depraved maniac was loose and roaming their streets. But that's not what happened.

There was no outcry of forcing the police to open a new investigation. There was no group of vigilantes scouring the area looking for the person who assaulted Amanda. Instead, the county returned to its normal routine and no one else was ever charged.

• • •

It goes without saying that I could never be part of a jury that had anything to do with child abuse, child molestation, or anything that had to do with someone so young and innocent being hurt. My bias and prejudices could not be contained, but our system is what it is. We have to accept the not guilty verdicts and move on. Someone or multiple people in that sleepy town know the truth, but it's very likely they will go to their graves with the knowledge of what happened.

Depending on your belief system, you could be of the persuasion that the person or persons who did this to Amanda will face a much higher court one day. That on the day of their final judgement, they will not be able to hide behind a *Not Guilty* verdict or for never having been charged with the crime at all.

If you are of another persuasion, you believe in karma and know in the bottom of your heart that no one would be able to get away with what was done to Amanda from a philosophical perspective. As the old saying goes, 'Karma's a bitch.'

In the end, I have to believe that justice will prevail. Just not the way those associated with the trial would have wanted it to.

Chapter 7

As Jennifer and I were gathering information for Amanda's story, we went to the courthouse where the trial was held. I could see how it pained her to relive those moments, but it was helping her recall those early days when Amanda became part of our lives. As we stood on the courthouse steps, she started to talk about how it had felt to sit there day after day and process the testimony that was being presented.

"You know, Mom, it wasn't easy to listen to the evidence, and was even harder to hear the words that came out of the mouth of the defense attorney. I think I'm too much like you. Can't imagine ever being on a jury and not having my bias in favor of the victim."

Her eyes were starting to water, and I was very familiar with the look that was on her face. She was deep in memory and overcome by sadness. "There are some things I don't think I am ever going to understand. In some ways, I worried that I had failed Amanda during the trial. I don't really know what I could have done, but when the judge told me I wasn't allowed to bring her into the courtroom, I was angry.

"He said that the jury seeing Amanda would taint their ability to listen to the evidence with an open mind. I know she was a minor, just having turned four, but I felt her rights were being violated."

I can never recall a time when I saw my daughter angry in her entire life, but when it came to Amanda, the 'momma bear' that is in all of us reared its head, stood on her hind legs and would easily defend her daughter with every ounce of courage she had. She was prepared to fight to the death if need be.

"I often wanted to ask Bill why he accepted the judge's decision on that, but life is so much easier when we are looking back instead of being in the moment. What's that old saying, 'Hindsight is 20/20?' " she asked.

"Yep, I know exactly what you mean," I said. "Wish I knew what I know now with so many of the decisions I've made in my life. Maybe I wouldn't have made all the mistakes that I have."

God knows my daughters had seen me make my share, but the one thing that I had always hoped they would learn from me is that it is okay to make a mistake. The trick to life is to not keep repeating them.

"So what do you remember most about the trial?" I asked assuming it would be something about the testimony of key witnesses or the opening or closing arguments.

"That's an easy one to answer," she said, then crossed her arms across her chest and let out a heavy sigh. "What I remember most is standing right here on this very step. I don't remember what part of the trial we were in, but after we had broken for lunch, I was standing here talking to a couple of friends who had come to support me during the proceedings."

Her 'feisty' was starting to show as she continued. "You know how sometimes you sense that someone is just lurking in the background and waiting for the people around you to leave so that they can say something?" she asked.

"That happens all the time at work," I said. "They don't want anyone else to hear what they want to tell you or maybe are too embarrassed to ask in front of others."

Her eyes closed and I could tell she was going back to that moment. "When I was standing here waiting for the trial to resume, Amanda's biological mother, Tammy, came up to me. I knew who she was because of her testimony. She and I had never been formally introduced. It really was quite awkward."

I could only imagine. I wondered if there was a part of her that wanted to scream at Amanda's biological mother and ask, "How could you have let this happen to your baby? How could you have not known that the man you were trusting to care for Amanda was a potential monster or that the jealousy of a scorned ex-wife could have led to that beautiful baby losing her ability to function as a normal person?"

But Jennifer was not like that. She wasn't going to assign blame—that was for the courts to decide. She wasn't going to get angry with God for letting this happen to Amanda. All she knew then was that she would do anything and everything in her power to give Amanda the best life she could.

She paused momentarily, trying to piece together the encounter. "I can't tell you the exact moment that I fell in love with Amanda. It was somewhere between that first meeting and going to pick her up to bring her home. But in my heart, I knew that she belonged with Paul and me. Can't imagine our family any other way."

Her face became soft and tender. It was easy to see she was remembering those first few days with Amanda. "But I can tell you the exact moment that I knew she was going to be a part of our lives forever."

She stopped again. The memories were strong and the emotions were bubbling over. "As I said, it was easy to tell that Tammy wanted to talk to me. In many ways, I was hoping that my friends would close ranks and not let her get to me, but other people got their attention, and the next thing I knew, I was face to face with her.

"She asked if I knew who she was and Mom, you would have been proud of me. Part of me wanted to be condescending and snooty and say, 'Of course I do,', but you didn't raise me that way. I know there had to be a part of her that was aching in a way I couldn't imagine."

She was trying to get past her reactions to the memory, but I could tell how challenging it was to recall the scene that was playing out in her mind. "Her baby was never going to be the same. She was never going to have the life that she dreamed of for Amanda. Within a split second, my defenses dropped and compassion took over, but common sense didn't take a back seat." She grinned because she knew I would get her meaning.

"So my dear daughter, are you saying that regardless of the circumstance, you will let logic prevail? Guess making you watch all those episodes of Star Trek finally paid off." We both laughed.

"Yes, I guess you can say it did. Tammy asked me how Amanda was doing. I told her she was fine and that she was making some progress."

Progress for Amanda was now measured very differently. It wasn't as if she would ever regain control of her arms and legs or be able to hold a conversation. But Jennifer had gotten her to where she could eat 'real' food, as long as it was ground to the consistency of baby food. She had worked with the school to start Amanda on a program to recognize words as well as teaching her to understand sign language as a means of communicating. And Amanda never tired of having her daddy, Paul, sign her name. Some of her biggest grins where when his fingers spelled out her name: A-M-A-N-D-A.

"But then Mom, she said something that made me go into a protective mode that I had no idea I was capable of. She said she was thinking of trying to get custody of her and take her back.

"It may not have been my finest moment, and maybe I should have shown a little more compassion." She stopped before continuing. Her warrior spirit that I loved so much showed itself. "I looked her straight in the eye and said *'I'll fight you for her.'*" Jennifer was smiling slightly, but with a tinge of sadness for the pain she knew another human being was feeling.

"Tammy looked at me and said 'That's all I needed to know.' It was kind of eerie because she just turned and walked away. I think she just needed to hear that Amanda was loved, and I think it helped her to know we would do anything to keep her."

There are so many moments in life when we wonder if we are failing as parents. Then there are those moments when we see our children step up and soar beyond our wildest expectations.

I have had so many of those moments as I've watched not only my daughters, but all my grandchildren be better people because of Amanda. She has taught all of us the true meaning of accepting people for who they are. She has inspired them to love without expectations.

Chapter 8

It should be noted that Amanda's day-to-day life was as nondescript as the next person's. We get up, wash our faces, brush our teeth, take a shower, have breakfast, and head off to school or work. We come home, cook dinner, watch TV, or attend some after-school activity as either a participant, sibling, or parent. We repeat that same pattern day after day.

For a little girl whose physical abilities were severely limited, her impact on others was significant. A year after the 'incident,' the small town came together again because of Amanda. The trial was over and the verdicts had been rendered, but the legacy of Amanda was just beginning.

I remember the phone conversation with Jennifer after she and Paul were the guest speakers at the first anniversary meeting of the Family Resource Network that was started because of what happened to Amanda. "So how did the meeting go last night?" I asked.

"Mom, it was scary at first. I didn't know how people were going to react to Amanda. And for some reason, the sight of a wheelchair can really make people uncomfortable."

There was a distinct sadness in her voice as she spoke about how some people stare or quickly avert their eyes trying not to see the handicapped individual.

"When we entered the room, people were chatting, laughing, and exchanging pleasantries as they drank their coffee, tea, or hot chocolate and nibbled on the cookies. But the room went totally quiet as soon as they noticed us. For a minute there, I really wanted to turn around and walk out."

It was a brand new life for Amanda, but it was also a brand new life for Jennifer and Paul. The story of what happened to Amanda followed them everywhere they went. Small towns are like that. Everyone knew them as the couple who had taken in the little girl in the headlines.

I could hear Jennifer let out a sigh before she continued with her story. "The first thing we did was take Amanda out of her wheelchair. You know how much she loves it when she is in Paul's lap. She would look at him, then at me, and every now and then, she would flash that smile at the audience. You could tell she melted their hearts the same way she has ours.

"I was stunned to see the tears in people's eyes as I was recounting how Paula had called almost fifty different facilities and foster homes before she found us, making the story even sadder.

"But I explained the challenges we have faced. How frustrating it can be at times because you don't know how to help your child, but how in the same moment, every step forward makes it all worthwhile."

"Did you hear what you just said?" I asked.

Since we were talking on the phone, I could only imagine the look of puzzlement on her face. "What do you mean?" she asked.

"Do you remember the conversations we had when you and Paul were trying to make the decision of whether to take on the responsibility of caring for Amanda?"

With the hint of a laugh in her voice, she said, "Mom, I don't remember ten minutes ago sometimes with everything I have to do to take care of Amanda. You warned me to watch out for mommy brain, and now I know exactly what you mean."

"Jennifer, I told you that when you were making the decision to take her into your home, it would never matter to you that you didn't give birth to her. That love grows in our hearts more than it grows in our bellies.

"You were explaining how your life has changed since Amanda became part of your world. You didn't sugar coat the challenges that you have faced. But now you are talking to fifty plus strangers about caring for *your* daughter."

"Mom, I guess you are right. I didn't give birth to her, but I can't imagine life without her now. There was a time when I wasn't sure if she was ever going to smile, but now when I see those dimples and the twinkle in her eyes...." She paused and I could tell she was trying to hold back the tears.

"But when she smiles at either Paul or me, when I see her react to the hugs we give her...." Again she paused. "All I can say is that it is exhilarating. All the money in the world doesn't amount to the riches of that smile."

I knew how she felt. I had the same feelings about both her and her sister, and now I was learning a whole new level of love with the addition of Amanda to our family.

"Jennifer, I have a feeling that everyone in that room understood the depth of your and Paul's love for her. It's more than taking in a little girl who needed a family. It's about the power of love. It can work miracles. I have no doubt that we will all see the marvels life has to offer through Amanda's smile."

Chapter 9

As the weeks turned into months, and the months turned into years, Jennifer and Paul's family continued to grow. In 1997, they added a second child to their family.

Rodney was a special needs infant whom they welcomed into their home when he was six weeks old. His story wasn't as traumatic as Amanda's, but it is sad nonetheless.

It was rumored that he was born to an alcoholic, diabetic, woman in her forties who neglected to get even a minimal amount of prenatal care. Unfortunately from the onset, he didn't stand a chance for a normal life.

His disabilities included a severe cleft palate and lip as well as being blind and mentally challenged. Rodney, however, was the perfect baby.

He rarely cried, seldom fussed about anything, and loved to be cuddled—every grandmother's dream. I loved to watch him stretched out on a blanket on the floor where he would coo at the sound of voices and my off-key attempts at singing. His outbursts of uncontrolled laughter brought visions of cherubs circling around him playing peek-a-boo or gently tickling him with a feather.

I would be lying if I didn't say that I had some concerns about the challenges that having two kids with such limited functionality would bring to any relationship. It was not just the day-to-day care that was required. Both children would need multiple surgeries over the coming years. Rodney to correct the cleft palate and lip. Amanda to have a pump implanted to deliver medication to relieve the pain of her ever-stiffening muscles as well as back surgery to correct the curvature of her spine.

One might think that having two special needs children would deter Jennifer and Paul from having a biological family, but it was still something they hoped to experience as well. I can't say having children of their own, because to them, Amanda and Rodney were their own kids. Jennifer, however, often joked throughout the years that the eight day method of becoming a parent was much easier than the nine month conventional way.

A few months after welcoming Rodney into their home, Jennifer found out she was pregnant. I was beaming at the news, but concerned with the daunting task of them having the equivalent of three infants from a care perspective. My momentary doubt was replaced with knowing that if anyone could pull it off, it was the two of them.

As the due date for my third grandchild, Justin, was approaching, I was concerned with being able to be there for his birth. Because babies rarely come on their due date, I eventually made a reservation to fly into Clarksburg, WV on Saturday, October 24 thinking that I would arrive before Jennifer went into labor. Justin however had other plans, and arrived two days before I got there.

I remember getting the call when Justin was born. He was a beautiful little boy, perfect in every way from an outward appearance, but healthy he wasn't. What I recall most about those forty-eight hours before I arrived in West Virginia were two conversations I had with Jennifer.

"Mom, they are moving Justin to Ruby Memorial in Morgantown. The nurse who was taking care of him after he was born noticed a problem, and he has to have surgery immediately or he isn't going to survive. Paul told me she was in tears when she broke the news. She said it could be fixed, but she just couldn't understand how of all the people in Buckhannon, our son would be born with a serious medical condition.

"The doctors won't release me to go to Morgantown. They said I've lost too much blood and am not strong enough to make a sixty-mile trip."

I felt helpless as I listened to my daughter sobbing over the phone. It broke my heart that I couldn't put my arms around her to comfort her. And I felt helpless because there was no way I could ease the emotional pain that she was feeling. Listening seemed so inadequate.

She composed herself enough to finally say what my heart felt. "Mom, why is this happening to us?"

I knew there was nothing I could say that would make it better. Saying I love you and that I would get there as fast as I could really didn't help matters. But being 1,300 miles away, it was all I could do.

I didn't sleep much that night. Partly because of the packing that I needed to do, but mostly because of the worry that had overtaken my being. I counted the hours before I could call Jennifer again and check on her and Justin.

They say we have a special bond with our children and often know how they are thinking. We don't always agree on everything, but in a crisis situation, we seem to be linked by some cosmic connection that has our thoughts on the same exact wave length.

After the perfunctory hellos, Jennifer and I said at the same time, "God is fair."

We laughed at the irony of saying the same thing in unison. "Jennifer, I think I know exactly why we both said that. Of all the people in that town, there are no parents better equipped to handle this type of situation.

"It's not going to be easy, but you and Paul know the right questions to ask. You know the drill of what is expected after a surgery. You know the signs to look out for as they pertain to unforeseen issues. You will stay calm in the face of adversity and you will hold it together," I said, hoping my words reassured her.

"I agree one hundred percent; this is going to be a challenge. They aren't going to release me until tomorrow," Jennifer said. "My friend Carrie is driving in from Cleveland as we speak. Michelle and her son Nathan are going to stay with Amanda and Rodney at the house, and Beth and Paul will be helping as well, so we can concentrate on getting Justin well.

"Carrie wasn't planning on coming until next week, but as soon as she heard what was going on, she decided to drive in. She will stay with me while Paul is in Morgantown with Justin. The two of us will pick you up at the airport on Saturday and then head to the hospital. Finding a room is next to impossible. These folks in West Virginia take their football as seriously as we do in Texas. WVU is playing Miami this weekend and they are expecting over 60,000 people at the game. The hospital was able to get us a room at the Ronald McDonald House. Only two twin beds, but we will make do."

It didn't help, but I told her to try not to worry. I would be there on Saturday and would be spending a couple of weeks to help with the process of settling in with a new baby. They would need even more help with Amanda and Rodney as they worked through the issues Justin faced.

Luckily, everything went well with the initial surgery, and within a few days, Jennifer and Paul were able to bring their second son home. Justin would need several more surgeries before he turned one, but for now they could get on with life and look forward to the adventures ahead.

Chapter 10

It is sad to say, but I've often noticed how individuals with handicaps are feared. It is no more rational than how most of us will flail our arms uncontrollably when we walk through a spider's web or jump up on the nearest table if we see a mouse. People will look away, cross to the other side of the mall, or cast their eyes downward so that they don't have to look the handicapped person in the eye.

One of the things Amanda has taught me is to smile at individuals with handicaps as well as the caregivers who are with them. It's something very simple, but I've often seen a sense of relief come over the caregiver when I smile at them. It's an unspoken sign that says, 'I understand.' It's an acknowledgment of the sacrifices they are making to give the handicapped person as fulfilling a life as they can.

Although some people were afraid of Amanda in the beginning, most people were drawn toward her. Maybe it was because she was so tiny. Maybe it was because she smiled at you regardless of what was going on. Most likely it was how her soul radiated from her beautiful blue eyes and her smile that welcomed you into her world.

This was especially true of the respite workers who helped take care of her. The majority of them have stayed in touch with the family and are now close friends. One of Amanda's favorites was Michelle—, but not for the reason you might think. Amanda loved Michelle, but she adored who came with her. As many young single moms have experienced, it isn't easy to have a job and be able to afford daycare. Jennifer and Paul understood the hardship of finding a babysitter in their small town, so they allowed Michelle to bring her three-year-old son with her when she needed to. Eight-year-old Amanda was smitten by the towheaded, blue-eyed little boy.

"Granny, I'm sooo glad you came to see me. It's been so long since you were here. I hate that we live sooo far away from you. But I'm just glad you are here now." I was amused how she drew out the word "so" in every conversation my mind had with her.

Her eyes were gazing across the room from one person to another. From the look on her face, I could see she had more to say. *"Did you see Michelle? She brought Nathan with her today. Isn't he the cutest little thing?"*

Her eyes focused on the playful antics of this little boy. She grinned watching him play with his toys. *"I know I'm five years older than him, but he always wants to play with me. Earlier, he was running that big red fire truck up the side of my chair, then over my lap and down the other side.*

"It kind of tickled. He's a little noisy sometimes, but he loves to show me his favorite toy of the day. Sometimes he just piles all the cars and trains in my lap."

I could hear the chuckle in her voice. It was easy to tell how much it meant to her as he toddled over and tried to put his favorite book in her hand.

"I know in the beginning, right after the 'incident,' most people didn't do many things with me. They would smile and say hello, but I think they were a little afraid of me. Didn't really have a chance to get to know other kids.

"First, it was the trial, and then there was so much new stuff that Mom and Dad were working on with me.

"Nathan isn't like the other kids I'm around. He is actually my first friend." The love she had for this little boy was touching.

"Sometimes he starts pushing me around in my chair, and 'the moms' kind of freak out." Her eyes were rolling and twinkling as she filled in the details.

"They need to understand I'm not fragile. I can handle a bump or a bruise. I'm tougher than I look," she said with exasperation.

And then her mood changed. It wasn't unhappiness that I sensed. It was an acceptance of her situation coupled with frustration. *"I wish they understood. Nathan makes me..."* She paused to make sure she found the right words. *"He makes me feel normal."*

She smiled and continued, *"You know Granny, I'm really glad you are here. It was nice of you to come see us and meet my little brother. I heard Mom and Dad talk about how he was going to have to have a lot of surgeries—just like Rodney and me, but for different reasons."*

She seemed to hesitate for a few minutes with her thoughts. I wondered if part of her was afraid to express her fears, but when she continued, I was touched that she felt safe to share her feelings. *"I have to be honest, I was worried for a few minutes if Mom and Dad would still want Rodney and me, once they had kids of their own. I understand that is normal for those of us that are in foster care. Everyone wants a forever home."*

But then her frown turned into a smile as she decided the self-doubt wasn't worth her time. *"I'm sooo excited every time they bring my baby brother over for me to hold. He's a squirmy little guy. Granny, I am sooo lucky. We may not be a conventional family, but we are a family nonetheless.*

"I know my life is not the same as when I was three, but I do know I am loved. I wonder where I would be if I wasn't with Mom and Dad."

"Amanda, you will never be replaced in your parents' hearts. They love you unconditionally as do the rest of us. You will always be my Panda girl," I said, then giving her a kiss on the cheek. "I wish we didn't live so far apart either. I'll only be able to stay a couple of weeks and then have to head back to Houston. But I'm going to try and help your Mom.

"If nothing else, I can fill her freezer with food. I know she wants me to make her some gumbo, and I'm going to make that chicken dish and my lasagna that you like so much. "And don't forget, you all will be coming to Houston for Christmas which is only two months away."

Her eyes brightened at the thought of the holiday season, and her smile returned when I asked, "Do you want to help me with the cooking?" She was grinning from ear to ear knowing she could help make her favorite dishes. And she was even more excited to now have two little brothers. But then her face contorted and the smile turned mischievous.

"Justin is really sweet and Rodney is such a hoot sometimes. But do you think you can talk to Mom and let her know I really, really, really want a baby sister?"

I laughed out loud. She loved her brothers, but the idea of having someone to play dolls with or someone who could paint her nails was something that only a sister could do with her.

Eight years later, Jennifer and Paul welcomed another son, Joseph, into the family. As soon as Amanda saw his face, she fell in love instantly and the idea of wanting a baby sister was temporarily forgotten. She was thrilled that Justin was going to have a brother to play ball and video games with.

Chapter 11

As the years rolled by, the beauty and tranquility of the area couldn't replace being close to family. Jennifer and Paul loved the advantages that small town living provided, but something was missing. They had established themselves in the community. Friendships had been formed and Paul had tenure, but the 1,300 mile trek at Christmas time and during the summer was becoming more and more challenging. Not to mention the almost 2,200 miles it took to visit Paul's family in Calgary.

With Amanda and Rodney both in wheelchairs and getting larger every day, changing and feeding them was becoming almost impossible to do in a van. Add a very rambunctious typical little boy into the mix, and it was obvious that those long drives could not continue.

It was after a lot of soul searching that they eventually came to the conclusion that it was time to move closer to family. They would miss their friends and the life they had created. But with the prospect of aging on the horizon for a number of grandparents and parents, they felt it was best to be within a four to five hour drive from Jennifer's side of the family if possible. The trip to visit Paul's family wouldn't be much shorter, but it would save many thousands of miles on the road each year.

Moving for the Withey family was about more than Paul finding a new job. Amanda and Rodney were technically wards of the state so taking them out of West Virginia would require a new arrangement. And giving up their children was not an option.

The concerns Jennifer and Paul had weren't about the help they were getting with the day to day needs such as diapers, clothes, and food. There concerns were centered around the medical problems that lay ahead for both children. The pre-existing conditions and future medical issues that both Amanda and Rodney faced would probably not be covered under any insurance program available through potential employers.

After many discussions with Child Protective Services, the decision was made that the best alternative was adoption. They were fortunate that the state was willing to work out an arrangement to help with basic needs, as well as covering both children with medical insurance until they turned twenty-one when Medicaid would take over. The upside to the plan was that adoption formalized what we all knew in our hearts. Amanda and Rodney were family and always would be. Adoption was only a technicality.

With the details of the adoption issues in the works, Paul began looking for teaching jobs in Texas, Louisiana, Arkansas, Mississippi, Alabama, and Oklahoma. He had several possibilities, but in the end, he chose Northwestern State University in Natchitoches, LA. This meant that the Withey clan would be four to five hours from both sets of Jennifer's parents, grandparents, and great-grandparents. Driving time to Paul's family in Canada, would be a little shorter, but not by much.

As they say, timing is everything, and the formal adoption took place the day before they were scheduled to start the trek to Louisiana. The proceedings reunited three of the key players from Amanda's trial. Paula, the social worker who placed Amanda in their home, was handling the state side of things for both children. Bill, the attorney who prosecuted Amanda's case, now had a private practice and would represent Jennifer, Paul, and the kids. The judge, who officially signed the papers for the state concerning the legal formation of this new family, had presided over Amanda's trial. In many ways, it was a partial happy ending to what had been a very traumatic event in all of their lives.

• • •

Just as professional poker players get to know their opponents, Amanda had a 'tell' that was undeniable when she was overcome with happiness. Her eyes shone just a little brighter, and both corners of her mouth turned up, and the indentation of her dimples recessed even further into her cheeks.

"Granny, I'm sooo happy you came to help us move. I'm going to miss Michelle and Nathan, but it is going to be sooo nice to be close to all of you.

And similar to a peacock strutting and displaying its feathers, the pride that she felt showed when she said, *"And today, Rodney and I officially become part of the family."*

I gave her a hug, softly whispering, "Sweetheart, you have been part of this family since the day your parents met you. We wouldn't be the same without you."

"I know. I never doubted that Mom and Dad would always be there for me. But I have to say, there is something special about making this legal; it makes me sooo happy."

The sense of relief I felt from her and for myself was not something I expected. She would always be a part of our family. We would never decide to not take care of her, but knowing that the state could never take her back brought a pleasure I didn't expect.

I wish I could say I remember a lot about the adoption ceremony itself, but my recollection of the courtroom was overshadowed by the memories of the breakfast we had afterwards.

The newly formed Withey family made its way to the local diner along with Bill, Paula, Jennifer's dad, better known as Gramps, and me. Needless to say, we made an entrance, especially with pushing two wheelchairs—something we were very used to.

Other patrons, however, would often be caught off guard. Sometimes it would make them uncomfortable. Sometimes it would elicit stares of wondering what happened that a family would have two handicapped children. Other times it tugged at a person's heartstrings seeing this young couple taking care of not one, but two needy children and a toddler.

During this meal, it was definitely the latter. The elderly gentleman seated at the next table started a conversation with Paul. It's understandable that most people are curious when they see a family with two handicapped kids, but seldom do they have the nerve to ask what happened.

As Paul explained that we had just gotten back from court to finalize Amanda and Rodney's adoption, the man was overcome with emotion. He understood how a family takes care of children when they are born into the situation, but he was in complete awe of these two parents who had actually chosen to take on the responsibility of two severely handicapped individuals.

As he finished his breakfast, he paid his bill and then came over to the table. He extended his hand to Paul and said, "God bless you and your wife. You have shown me the true meaning of being a Christian. Please take this as a token of gratitude for doing the work of the Lord."

Paul thanked him and assumed that the bill he felt in his hand would be a five, ten, or twenty dollar bill. But as the man walked away, Paul unfolded the money. To his surprise, the man had given him a $100 bill. The money would go a long way with the move and would help ease some of the financial concerns that were overshadowing the trip.

• • •

The part of the day that left me heartbroken was my conversation with Bill. As we walked out of the diner, I had a chance to briefly speak with him as I hadn't been sitting next to him at the table in the restaurant.

"Thank you so much for doing this for Jennifer and Paul. It means so much to them that you were a part of the final step in this journey."

He looked at me and smiled while saying, "It truly was my pleasure. You have an incredible daughter and son-in-law. Don't think I have ever met finer people in my life." His words were genuine. The respect he had for Jennifer and Paul and the challenges they had taken on were obvious.

"I'm pretty fond of them myself," I said, beaming with pride. "I hope that handling the adoption has brought the story of Amanda to a close for you. And knowing that she is going to be with a family that loves her forever brings you closure." I let out a heavy sigh. This was the end of one chapter, but the beginning of a new one for this blended family.

He hesitated before speaking, his eyes filling with tears. "Yes, it does bring closure in one sense. I can rest knowing that Amanda is loved by so many. It wasn't just Jennifer and Paul who accepted her into their lives, but all of their extended family as well."

He turned his face away briefly, his shoulders slumped, and his breathing labored by the knot that was in his throat. "I..." He stopped again. "I think about that trial so often. I have second-guessed myself so many times. I've played every moment over and over in my head. I have often wondered what I could have done differently, but at the end of the day..." His voice was cracking. I wasn't sure he was going to continue. "At the end of the day, I will never forgive myself. I failed to get justice for Amanda." He shook his head as the tears rolled down his face. "I'll never forgive myself," he said again.

My heart ached for him. I wanted to tell him that justice will one day be served. That regardless of the outcome of the trial, there was a higher judgment that awaited the person who hurt Amanda.

I have no doubt that when that day comes, the person or persons who was responsible for brutalizing this beautiful little girl or who helped assure a Not Guilty verdict will wish they had paid for their sins on this plane.

• • •

As we gathered back at the house to do the final packing, the excitement of the pending move was growing to a fevered pitch. Several friends came to help, and all of their belongings were loaded into the van before the sun set.

"Granny, this is sooo exciting! I can't believe we will soon only be a couple of hours from you, Aunt Cia, Gramps, and Gran." The excitement of the day and the upcoming move were not lost on Amanda. *"The only thing that makes me sad is that I won't get to see Nathan anymore like I do now."*

"I know, sweetie. It is hard when we have to move away from our friends. But Michelle and Nathan are going to make the trip with us and stay for a week. You will have lots of time to play with him. And maybe he will get a chance to come see you sometimes."

"I certainly hope so. It will make me sad not to see him a few times a week, but I'm going to look on the bright side. I now get to see you and the rest of the family more often."

Thankfully, the trip to Louisiana was uneventful. Our caravan of cars made the trip in record time. All that was left now was to start the unpacking as a whole new life lay in front of them. There would be new schools, new friends, and a whole new set of experiences.

But one thing didn't change. And that was Amanda's effect on the people she would come in contact with in this brand new city.

Chapter 12

Contrary to stories that people post on Facebook, Twitter, Instagram, or Snapchat, life is more the kiddie train jaunt around the park than it is a 24-7 roller coaster ride. But every now and then, we find ourselves in the middle of an event that borders on extraordinary.

Although Amanda's likeness and the story of her life was no stranger to the front page, I don't think any of us thought that her picture would ever grace a newspaper again. But events were unfolding in Florida which would change that.

Amanda wasn't the headline of the story, but her appearance in Pinellas Park would be captured by several photographers. A few of those photos found their way to the front page of several Florida newspapers and were distributed across the AP wire.

• • •

It was March 2005, and Jennifer, Paul, and the kids were in town for the funeral of the father of my now ex-husband. We were standing in the parking lot at a local restaurant in west Houston, having had lunch after the service.

There wasn't much unusual about the day. It was typical Houston March weather. Sun was shining; skies were blue with just a few thin clouds. We were all enjoying the two weeks of spring that we cherish here in the Deep South. Everyone knew it was just a matter of days before the temperatures would start climbing above ninety again and summer would be in full swing.

As we were standing around chatting, Paul mentioned the Terri Schiavo situation that was currently capturing the attention of the nation. "Can you believe that the courts are actually agreeing with her husband? I can't imagine what they are thinking," he said shaking his head.

"I haven't seen the news in days. We have been a little preoccupied with the arrangements for the funeral. What's going on?" I asked.

Jennifer chimed in with details. "There is a young woman in Florida whose husband petitioned the courts to stop giving his wife water or nourishment. Her diagnosis is that of a persistent vegetative state. But Mom, every time I see the news clips of Terri, I see Amanda. Her reactions to her surroundings, as well as the smile that she has on her face when she hears the voices of her loved ones, all remind me of how Amanda reacts to her environment.

"I really don't get it. Neither one of them is being kept alive by machines. They have to be fed and cared for similar to infants, but Amanda has a full life. It may not be what we would have wanted for her, but we are doing everything we can to give her as many opportunities and experiences as possible."

I put my arm around her as I could see she was visibly shaken just by telling me the story. "It's going to be okay. I can't imagine that any court would be so cruel as to starve a woman to death."

The sadness in her eyes told me she wasn't nearly as optimistic as I was.

"I don't know. From what I'm hearing, it doesn't look good. I wish they could see Amanda and recognize how precious life is. I can't imagine anyone ever telling me that Amanda's life isn't worthwhile." Now the tears were flowing freely down her face.

"So why can't they see her?" I asked.

"You mean Paul and I should take Amanda to Florida?"

The one mind syndrome that the two of them shared started clicking. One could see the wheels turning as they non-verbally exchanged thoughts.

"Why not? Your sister and I can take care of Rodney and Justin. I'll take a few more days off work if I need to. What's stopping you from going? You never know how one act might change everything."

I opened my wallet and took out some cash. "Here's some money for gas and food. Take Amanda. Do what you have to do. And we can all pray that sanity will prevail."

We went back to my house where we started preparing for their journey to Florida. They had driven in from Louisiana and would leave from Houston, so we did a load of laundry and repacked their bags. They would leave for Florida early the next day.

• • •

Their first stop was in Tallahassee at the governor's office. They tried to get an audience with Governor Jeb Bush, but were only able to meet with one of his aides. He assured them that he would pass along Amanda's story.

In between taking care of my grandsons, I was glued to the TV. I wondered if I would get a glimpse of the three of them in the background of some reporter's on camera interview. But what I was really hoping for was that the media would interview them. Anyone who saw Amanda would immediately make the connection between these two women and their conditions.

My vigilance and channel flipping finally paid off. I was ecstatic when Amanda's smile filled the TV screen. My prayers had been answered. Jennifer and Paul were being interviewed by a reporter from CNN while they walked the capital grounds.

They were explaining the similarities between Amanda's diagnosis and Terri's to the reporter. They focused on all the positive experiences Amanda had received since she became part of the family. How even though her interaction was limited because she could not speak, she communicated through her eyes and her smile, both of which inspired others.

The bond and love that these two parents and their daughter shared was unquestionable. They had been the three musketeers since the first day they met almost ten years earlier. As they left the capital, they were in high hopes. They trusted that when people saw Amanda, they would understand the value of every life regardless of a person's limitations.

Their next stop was Pinellas Park. The media was camped out in full force. Reporters from CNN, FOX News, and every major outlet were keeping vigil and reporting on the current situation. It was nonstop rehashing of the battles that had been going on in the courts for almost fifteen years between Michael Schiavo and the Schindler family.

People were commenting on both sides of the issue. One group was making the argument that 'it's not a life in that state' while others were chanting 'everyone has the right to food and nourishment' regardless of their diagnosis.

The fact that there was no will stating Terri would not want to live in her current state was outweighed by hearsay conversations that Michael Schiavo said he had with Terri. The evidence presented by the Schindler family regarding Terri's wishes as well as multiple doctors stating that the PVS diagnosis was incorrect were disregarded by the courts. Also ignored were the statements from some in the medical profession that stated Terri could have benefited from ongoing rehabilitation and therapy. The media played up the fact that Terri was on life support, but often stopped at that statement, misleading many to assume that she was tied to machines to breathe and keep her heart pumping. The 'life support' that Terri was receiving was feeding and hydration through a tube, just like Amanda.

Very few people I know haven't made the comment at some point in their life that they wouldn't want to live if they were tied to life support. Most of us, however, don't go in-depth and talk about other life sustaining procedures such as being fed by a tube. But death is not a topic, most of us are willing to talk about in detail. We think if we ignore the subject, it will just go away, but that's not the case. As the saying goes, there are only two things that none of us escape—death and taxes.

In some ways, my heart understands how painful it must have been for Michael Schiavo to watch the woman he once loved lose her ability to function. What I will never understand is why he didn't relinquish care of Terri to her parents. He was living with another woman and had two children with her. He had moved on with his life.

Why Michael Schiavo dug his heels in, and refused to see the other side of the story, is hard to understand. Many of us are guilty of having done the same thing at some point in our lives. But a woman's life was at stake, and it would have cost him nothing to let her family take care of her.

There is so much to this case and the legal battles put forth by both parties certainly must have taken their toll in more ways than one. I don't have all the facts. Only those involved know what happened to cause such diametrically opposing views. In the end, Michael and the courts that sided with him are ultimately responsible for their actions.

I think, however, that Amanda's presence was appreciated by the Schindler family. Terri's brother and father both came out and talked with Amanda. The picture that landed Amanda on the front page of the newspaper, was Bob Schindler, Terri's dad, talking to Amanda. He identified with Amanda's condition and cognitive capabilities. He and his family recognized that what others saw as blank stares was much more as the eyes of their loved one latched onto their every move. They understood the unspoken words.

• • •

When they returned, I sat with Amanda and asked her what she thought. Patting her hand and smiling, I said, "So now you are a full-fledged activist. How does it feel?"

"Granny, I can't believe what was going on there. There were so many people and they had completely different views of the situation. Sometimes they were yelling and screaming at each other. Some thought that it was cruel to let Terri live in that condition, but others were praying and saying how precious life is."

She stopped and took a deep breath. *"I, more than anyone, understand that."* She hesitated before continuing, obviously deep in thought. *"This may not be an ideal life, but I've been given so much love since the 'incident.' I don't think my biological mother could ever have loved me as much as Mom and Dad do.*

"Plus I have my brothers, aunts, uncles, cousins, and so many friends. I'm still amazed at how all the kids now fight over who is going to push my wheelchair at school." She was gushing with pride at that thought. Her eyes shined with happiness as she talked about her friends.

But then the sadness returned to her face. *"I heard one lady talking to Dad. She didn't think I understood her, but I did. When she looked at me, I could see the disgust on her face. Why do people not realize that I have feelings too?"* The pain in her eyes was unmistakable.

"Can you believe she said it was cruel to continue feeding me? That no one would want to live in this condition. I couldn't do any more than make

my normal grunting sounds, but I used every bit of brain power I had to try and tell her she was wrong."

I was mortified at the thought that my beautiful fourteen-year-old granddaughter would have to endure such hostility and hatred from someone she didn't even know. Unfortunately, I doubted it would be the last time. But true to form, Amanda didn't let it get her down.

The smile returned. "*Terri's dad came out and talked to me. He was so nice. He said he was so happy that I was there and that our support meant so much to him and his family. I could tell that he saw how similar our conditions were. He told me how lucky I was to have such an incredible mom and dad. I wanted to reach out and give him a big hug, but regrettably, these arms just don't work.*"

It was as if I could see her shoulders shrug and knew how much she wished she had control of her body. "B*ut I think he knew that I would if I could*" were the words I heard.

She continued telling me about her trip. "*Several reporters snapped a picture of me with Terri's dad. It was part of a story that was printed by the Tampa Bay Times, and I'm told was distributed on the AP wire, but I'm not really sure what that means.*

"*Granny, this is not how I would have wanted to be famous. But I truly hope that someone sees my picture and understands how much people in my condition want to live. Just because we aren't like everyone else doesn't mean we can't enjoy the life we do have.*"

I was taken aback by the depth of passion I saw in her eyes. She truly understood the gravity of the situation and how it could affect so many people.

"I have no doubt that Mr. Schindler did, Manda Panda. Let's just pray that sanity prevails. That Terri's feedings are reinstated and her family is given the right to take care of her."

A quick internet search will provide the details of the legal battles that went on for years. Regrettably, the courts never backed down and all the legal maneuvering that the Schindler family tried came to an end when Terri passed away on March 31, 2005.

I wasn't with Amanda when the news broke, but something tells me that as she listened to the broadcast of Terri's passing two tears must have trickled down her face. One of sadness that Terri was gone, and the other of happiness that she had a family that loved and was allowed to take care of her.

Chapter 13

After the trip to Florida, life went back to 'normal.' Or at least as normal as it can be for someone in Amanda's condition. For her, there was the residual pain that affected all of her muscles. Most days it didn't appear to be more than the equivalent of a mild headache. Others, it was obvious that the discomfort she felt was more than any child should have to bear. And although she would let us know when she wasn't feeling well, Amanda's focus was to share her smile.

It was her smile that endeared her to so many. It was something I felt personally and had seen on numerous occasions with others who got to know her, but her sixteenth birthday party was going to show all of us how deep an impact she had on the people who were a part of her life.

The idea for the party was hatched by Jennifer and revealed to her sister and me after Thanksgiving dinner in 2006. The under eighteen crew had cleared the table and the dads were loading the dishwasher and cleaning the kitchen.

We started planning our Black Friday shopping strategy when Jennifer looked at me with a mischievous expression on her face. I knew there was something brewing in her mind, but had no idea what it might be.

Knowing full well what my answer would be, she asked, "Mom, can you help me throw a Sweet Sixteen party for Amanda?"

My immediate response was 'of course,', but then I had to wonder how I was going to help her pull it off since we lived 250 miles apart. It would mean lots of phone calls to discuss plans and a few trips to Natchitoches over the next few months, but felt confident that we could make it happen. And needless to say, I would do whatever it took. Amanda was worth it and so much more.

"So what ideas have you come up with? Will we have it at your house? How many people are you planning to invite?" I asked.

"Was going to invite the whole town. That's not a problem for you is it?" Jennifer laughed as she saw me gasp.

"I know you girls kid me that I cook for an army, but I think that's a little out of my league. So really, what ideas have you come up with so far?"

"Let's just do something simple. Get some chicken from Popeye's, make potato salad, and maybe get meat pies from Lasyone's. We can fill in with lots and lots of appetizers — fruit and veggie trays and, of course, your queso. Wouldn't be a party without it." Jennifer smiled, knowing that I understood how important this was to her.

"I want to get a really pretty two-tiered cake and maybe have a few other dessert items. But what I really want to do is have sixteen people get up and tell everyone what Amanda has meant to them. What do you think?" She focused on my face to see my reaction.

"I love that idea. The hardest part is going to be narrowing it down to sixteen people. So many will want to say something about Amanda. You are going to have a hard time choosing who gets to speak. But as long as *I* can, I don't care about the rest." I laughed as I said it, but totally serious.

• • •

We decided we would start planning in earnest right after the first of the year. And plan we did.

Besides the details for the party itself, the second most important thing to Jennifer was finding a special dress for Amanda to wear.

The one thing I loved about Natchitoches was all the shops along Front Street that faced the Cane River. Every time we visited, I loved strolling through the antique, knick-knack, and kitchen stores that were interspersed with clothing, toy, and candy stores along with a few restaurants.

My favorite store was Kaffie Frederick's. Not many stores in the US sell everything from toilet plungers to Baccarat crystal to the best cast iron cookware you can find. On several occasions, they had a local artist, Grady Harper, exhibiting his watercolors depicting scenes from the area. My favorites, however, were the beautiful works of art that he painted using coffee.

The one thing I hated about shopping in a small Louisiana town was that there weren't many places to buy a party dress for a young girl. The lack of choices caused Jennifer to come up with a Plan B.

It was on a Monday evening about three weeks before the party when she called me. "Mom, what are you doing on Friday?"

"I thought I was going to be working, but something tells me there might be a plan in the works that I'm not aware of," laughing because I knew full well that she had an ulterior motive with her question.

"I was thinking that most girls Amanda's age would have found a way to skip school by now, so I thought we could help Amanda with that goal."

I could envision the smile on Jennifer's face because she knew I would have been mortified if I thought that either she or her sister had ever skipped school. She was taking great delight in making me break the rules. But she knew that when it came to Amanda, I would do anything.

"Can you and Marcia meet me in Lufkin? I thought we could go shopping for Amanda's Sweet Sixteen dress. I've looked everywhere here in Natchitoches, and I'm just not seeing anything that is going to work. I thought we could make it a girls' day out and see what we can find. And we would be helping Amanda with her badass image."

She was having way too much fun with her plan. But then I heard a serious tone that was a mixture of sadness and pride as she continued to fill me in on her ideas.

"I know she is never going to go to the prom. And I'll never have the experience of searching for the perfect wedding dress for her. But I really want her to have something special for her Sweet Sixteen party.

It's a special day, and I want her to feel like a princess."

I didn't hesitate with my answer. Any plans I had would have to be postponed. "Why don't we both leave around 8 am and meet at the mall in Lufkin? They have some of the bigger chains and probably a few specialty stores. I'm sure we will be able to find something that will be her dream dress. Does that work for you?" I asked.

"Sounds like a plan to me. You should see the smile Amanda has on her face right now. She's been listening to my side of the conversation. I know some people don't think that someone in her condition understands anything, but if they could ever meet her, they would see how she comprehends every word we say."

"Well, tell her that her aunt Cia and I will see her on Friday. We will find a dress as lovely as she is."

As I hung up the phone, I was struck by how quickly time passes. It seemed like just yesterday that Amanda was turning four, and a dozen years had now passed.

• • •

When we got to the mall, I called Jennifer and left her a voicemail that we would meet her in the food court at Chick-fil-A. I loved the drive to Natchitoches, but there had always been a large area between the two cities that was void of cell towers. I knew that as soon as she got into range her phone would notify her of my message so that she would know where to meet us.

I personally was ready for my first Diet Coke of the day, having gotten on the road at dawn. Marcia and I had made the 144 mile trip in record time. Mostly because of my lead foot.

I parked near the south entrance and we went inside to wait. Not being familiar with the mall, we decided to take a quick stroll to look for specialty shops and determine where the bigger anchor stores were located. We were thrilled when we saw a storefront that had bridal gowns, bridesmaid, and prom dresses.

Realizing that Jennifer and Amanda would be arriving shortly, we found our way back to the Chick-fil-A and ordered some nuggets for Marcia and a Diet Coke for me. "Okay, Mom, let's talk about this. Are you really going to try and do **all** of the food for the party? There's going to be close to a hundred people there. I can help, but do you really think we can get it all done?"

"You should know by now that my Cajun roots don't know how to cook for less than fifty people. We will be buying the chicken and meat pies and just supplying the sides and appetizers. I think we can do it. We've thrown some really big parties in the past, but this one is going to top all of those events." I wondered if the fake laugh masked my terror at being able to pull this off. But I really didn't have time to dwell on that thought. We needed to find a dress first.

The universe seemed to time their entrance with that thought. Right on cue, Jennifer strolled in pushing Amanda in her new yellow wheelchair. It was obvious that she was tired from the two-and-a-half hour trip, but a huge smile broke out on her face as soon as she saw us.

Amanda knew this day was all about her. And similar to most teenagers, she was going to take advantage of being the center of attention. There was a playful look on her face that I had not seen before.

"*Hi Granny. Are you ready to take me shopping?*" she asked, with a coy grin.

"You bet I am. Have you thought about the kind of dress you want? Something long and formal, or maybe something more casual?" I asked.

"*How about something low cut and really sexy and we find me some three-inch heels. That should make Mom crazy, don't you think?*" My mind heard her laugh out loud as she said the words.

"I think that's a great idea! Your mom and dad would 'have a cow'," joining in the laughter with her.

"*I'll know it when I see it. But you have to promise me you won't let Mom talk me into some boring dress. I want something that is going to make me feel beautiful. Something that says I'm sixteen, not six,*" she said as she rolled her eyes as only a teenager can.

Do you think we can find something that we all like?" she asked.

"I know we will find the right dress for you. Are you ready to start shopping?" I was going to be her ally in this venture and she knew it.

"*Yes, let's do this. I told my friend Heather that we were going shopping today. I can't wait to tell her about the dress. Once we find it, that is.*" She let out a huff.

"Granny, just promise me you will help convince Mom that it is the right dress when we find it. I'll let you know what I want to try on, but if I find THE ONE that is perfect, don't let anyone talk me out of it, okay?"

I knew how much this meant to her. She wanted the dress to be perfect for the party. Not so different from any other soon to be sixteen-year-old girl.

• • •

We tried the specialty shop first. We found a beautiful red dress that made Amanda's eyes light up, but when she put it on, the spark wasn't there. Then we went to the prom section of the Sears store. Again, there were a few things that got her attention, but it was obvious we hadn't found *the one* yet.

A few smaller shops didn't have any better selection, and I could see Amanda was starting to get discouraged. Group panic was starting to set in, and we all wondered what we would do if we couldn't find anything.

We had one more department store to try and that was JC Penney's. I could tell her energy was waning.

"Don't give up," I said to her as we walked to the other end of the mall.

She had been in her chair quite a while already, and I knew that tired her out.

"It takes a lot of looking to find the perfect outfit," I said, trying to reassure her.

As we started going through the racks of party dresses, I could tell that one caught her eye.

"Do you want to see that white one?" Her face contorted as if she were trying to say yes. I could only imagine how frustrated she must have felt not being able to verbally let us know what she wanted to try on.

"Jennifer, I think Amanda wants to see that white dress" pointing to one that was barely peeking through the overly-packed rack of clothes.

"This one?" she said pulling it out for all of us to see. As we all looked at Amanda, the smile that came across her face was all the confirmation we needed.

The dress was beautiful. It was white with one-inch navy blue polka dots all over it. The bodice had small navy piping across the top with navy spaghetti straps. The waist had a two-inch navy sash and the bottom had tulle that made it stand out.

"Do you want to try this one on?" Jennifer asked.

"Yes, pleassee. It is perfect! I know it is THE ONE!"

As Jennifer and Marcia took her into the dressing room, I anxiously waited by the door. Finding that dress had given Amanda a whole new burst of energy.

"Granny, are you ready to see the dress?" Marcia asked as she opened the door to push Amanda out to the three-way mirror.

Tears filled my eyes as I looked at her. She was no longer the sweet little girl that I shared Eskimo kisses with. She was what she always dreamed of being—a beautiful young woman with hopes and dreams like everyone else. She looked stunning and she knew it.

As she continued to gaze into the mirror, the happiness in her eyes was undeniable. The smile on her face told me everything and let me know how she felt. As her eyes met mine, she smiled again as I confirmed the approval of the dress.

"Granny, it's beautiful."

Chapter 14

As the day for her party approached, Amanda's excitement was spilling out everywhere. She knew this was going to be the biggest event of her life. She knew she was the center of attention and she relished every minute of it.

"Granny, can you believe my party is just three days away? Don't know how you and Mom are going to get all of this done."

She grinned and similar to any sixteen-year-old girl, she added, *"And I'm sooo worth it."* You could hear the giggle in her voice.

I laughed, seeing the twinkle in her eyes, but then watched as the expression on her face turned to concern.

"Seriously, Granny, we only have a few more days. Do you really think everything will be ready for the party?"

"Sweetheart, don't you worry about it. We ordered the cake and flowers last time I was here. See that big box of decorations over there. Your mom, aunt Cia, Gran Lindy, Leah, and Lauren are going to help me set everything up on Saturday morning. I'm going to go to the store tomorrow to get the food for the appetizers, so we will have plenty of time to get everything ready."

Didn't know if it would help, but I added, "I promise we are going to get it all done."

"I know you will do everything you can. But this is the biggest day of my life and the biggest party I will ever have.

*"I don't want you to think I'm feeling sorry for myself, but the truth is, we all know I'm never going to fall in love, have kids or any of the things that most people think of as a normal life. This is my moment...It needs.... no it **has** to be perfect!"*

She cast her eyes down for a moment before adding, *"I'm sorry I'm so stressed about this."*

My heart went out to her. It was the first time I had seen how aware she was of the restrictions of her physical condition. For the most part, she had adjusted her expectations about life accordingly.

"I know it is hard not to worry, but you have to know how excited we all are to be celebrating you. Your life may not have the same expectations as others, but the effect that you have on everyone you meet is rare. You change people in a way that the rest of us only wish we could."

She smiled, but it wasn't her normal smile. For the first time in years, it seemed as if her inabilities were getting the best of her. She was fretting over the details, but knew she couldn't do anything to help.

I stroked her arm and gave her an Eskimo kiss the same way I did when she was little. The sparkle reappeared, but with a small amount of reserve. "My love, I've never broken any of the promises I have made to you. Trust me when I say your day will be everything you dreamed it would be and more."

It's hard to say if she truly believed me, but her demeanor shifted from minor agitation to being relieved ever so slightly.

"Come help me bake some cookies for the party. Maybe there will be a few left if we can hide them from your dad and brothers," I said, then laughed.

Her smile softened and she welcomed the distraction of thinking about the party by helping me bake cookies.

"I trust you Granny. Let's make those cookies, and I'll help you find a hiding place.

• • •

As the decorating crew assembled the morning of the party, things were finally coming together. Tables were covered in pink cloths, and centerpieces of white and pink carnations adorned each one. Hershey Kisses and *Sweet 16* confetti had been sprinkled across them as well.

Buffet tables were set up along the back wall with pink and green paisley napkins, and plates. Light green plastic silverware was housed in pink-jeweled silverware caddies that I had found at Hobby Lobby.

We had printed a program detailing the events of the night staying with the pink and green color scheme. Each one had been rolled into a cylinder and tied with the opposite color of ribbon.

The theme of the party had been built around the centerpiece that Jennifer had put together using two separate candleholders. The first was a sixteen inch candle ring that had ten clear votive holders at alternating heights of one-half and one-inch. The second candle ring fit inside the larger one and had six tea light candles with a center vase for flowers.

A table was set up near the speaker's podium for the two cakes. It was covered with a white tablecloth and draped with a sheer pink-jeweled cloth that had been laid diagonally in the middle. The left side of the table held a two-tiered cake. The bottom had white icing adorned with pink and green trim. The top layer was light blue with **Sweet 16** written across the front. Two number candles—a 1 and a 6 — sat on top ready for her to blow out when the time came to sing 'Happy Birthday.'

The middle of the table held the sixteen-candle centerpiece. The vase was now filled with a spray of tiger lilies, baby's breath, and white roses. The right side of the table held sweetly-adorned cupcakes that were set in the shape of the number sixteen.

The friends and family members who would be speaking had been instructed about the order of events and their role. They were to tell the assembled guests what Amanda meant to them. There was no time limit on the speeches, and no direction on what they should say. Jennifer wanted everyone to speak from their hearts. Once they were done, they would light one of the candles in the centerpiece.

As expected, there was no shortage of people who volunteered to have one of the sixteen honored positions. From family members to respite workers (both current and past) to dozens of friends, everyone was hoping to be one of the chosen ones. They all had their stories ready to share.

Jennifer had a hard time narrowing down the list, but she eventually came up with a solution that was able to accommodate a large number of testimonials. For me, I wasn't concerned about what others were doing, because this was one time when being the 'granny' had its privileges. I was given the honor of going first.

At around 4 pm, the guests started to assemble. The mood was festive and the music was flowing. People were mingling and sharing stories about Amanda.

Finally, the time arrived for the testimonials to begin. I was starting to second-guess the honor of going first; the anxiety was creeping in. You would think that all the years of talking in front of crowds and teaching classes would have made this easier for me, but it wasn't. The right words needed to come out of my mouth.

I didn't have a written speech to follow, but I knew what I wanted to say. "Amanda, Amanda, Amanda. What can I say? I love all my grandkids equally, but there is something unique about the first grandchild.

"You elevated my status in the world to a whole new level. I had been a daughter and sister, then a wife, and by the grace of God, in 1972, I earned the moniker of 'Mom' when I gave birth to your mother.

"I didn't think anything would ever compare to the joy and ecstasy of holding either her or your aunt Cia in my arms for the very first time. But, boy, was I wrong.

"You didn't come into our world the 'normal' way. Unfortunately, we didn't have the honor of you being a part of our lives until you were about to turn four.

"You had a lot to overcome when you first joined our family, but you did it with a grace and dignity that most adults never have. You won us over with your smile. You filled our world with sunshine.

"It is so hard to believe that it has been twelve years since that first meeting, but here you are turning sixteen today. You have grown into an incredible young woman who speaks volumes with your eyes and inspires all of us with the smile that you give so freely. And you do it without ever asking anything in return.

"Your mom and aunt Cia taught me about unconditional love. But you, my dear, are the epitome of what it means to love and be loved unconditionally.

"I am both honored and humbled to be your granny.

"And now, with the tradition I started with your mom, I'm giving you a ring for your sixteenth birthday. I got this beautiful emerald-cut aquamarine—that matches the color of your eyes by the way—your birthstone—not long after you came into our lives. I've worn it over the years to fill it with love, hope, and courage knowing that one day I would place it on your finger.

"It seemed like it would be an eternity before I would give it to you, but in a blink of an eye, you went from four to sixteen. Know that when you wear it, I'm just a little closer; it will be a symbol of our bond.

"I love you, Panda Girl."

As I placed the ring on her finger, she flashed that smile that I had gotten so used to. She was proud to be the first of my granddaughters to carry on the tradition of the birthstone rings.

Tears were streaming down my face as I gave her a hug and then went to light the first of the sixteen candles.

Chapter 15

For most of us, we can't remember what we had for breakfast the day before, so remembering what everyone said at Amanda's party is not possible. But there were a few remarks that stood out which made a lasting impression on me.

The first was Amanda's friend Heather. It may seem odd to think of Amanda as having friends, but she did. And Heather's tribute spoke volumes about the meaning of friendship. As she stood in front of the crowd, decked out in her Star Wars t-shirt, cargo pants, and long straight brown hair flowing beneath an olive green cap, a smile came across her face.

"I've known Amanda for a few years now. It was scary at first because I had never been around anyone with a disability. But Amanda is my best friend now."

There were many in the room who questioned such a statement. Heather and Amanda didn't go to parties together, they didn't cruise the mall and hang out at the local burger joint, and more importantly, Amanda wasn't capable of carrying on the normal 'girl talk.' How could Amanda be her best friend?

"Amanda is definitely the quiet one in this friendship," she said with a chuckle in her voice. "And those of you who know me realize that works for me because I do have a tendency to talk a lot."

The guests laughed knowing how true a statement that was for any teenage girl.

"But friendships come in all shapes and sizes. And what makes a friendship isn't about sharing clothes or passing notes in class.

"Amanda is my best friend because she listens. She doesn't give me advice or tell me I should do something differently. But I do know by the look on her face if I've gone too far with my shenanigans."

The looks that the two were exchanging confirmed the depths of the friendship.

"Amanda is my best friend because I can tell her anything and she never judges me."

The crowd was now hushed in a way I hadn't seen the entire evening. The wisdom of this sixteen-year-old girl was coming through.

"Amanda is my best friend for all of the reasons I just mentioned. She is my best friend because I know she will never betray me. She will never talk behind my back, but more importantly, she will never share my secrets with anyone.

"Thank you Amanda for teaching me what true friendship means."

Amanda was beaming with happiness. She couldn't respond verbally, but the love that these two girls had for each other was unmistakable. It looked as if Amanda gave her a quick wink as Heather went to light her candle. She was acknowledging that her secrets were safe.

Another person who spoke was Amanda's friend Zack. He was a troubled kid in some ways because he wasn't fond of school or the work that was required. Jennifer had tutored him for a short period to help him catch up with his classes.

You could tell he was nervous, and there were a million places he would rather have been. Talking in front of a crowd was not his strong suit. But he wanted to be there for Amanda, so he would do what was needed to get himself through it.

He cleared his throat; he was ready to talk, but then hesitated. "Sorry folks. I didn't really prepare anything for tonight. Just thought I could get up here and wing it."

Those who knew him were shaking their heads. Wondering what it would take to get him to stop doing everything at the last minute.

But wing it he did.

"Amanda, you are one special person. My family and my friends refer to me as a 'Gloomy Gus.' I'm not one who smiles easily, and most of the time, I'm uncertain as to where I belong in this world. They tell me that is typical for most people my age. But knowing that doesn't make life any easier. What does make my life easier is seeing you.

"No matter how bad of a day I might have had, I can come into your house and you have a smile waiting for me. Your eyes are saying everything is going to be okay.

"I don't have this life thing down yet, but your smile helps me think beyond the norm. Your smile tells me that I can be a 'Gloomy Gus' with others, but with you, I have to enjoy life. With you, I have to make the best of what life has thrown at me because that is what you have done."

As he walked to the display to light his candle, he looked at Amanda and said, "Thank you for not letting me be a 'Gloomy Gus' around you."

Next up was Amy, who was studying to be a special education teacher. She had lived with Jennifer and Paul for several months while going to school and served as a respite worker during that time. Similar to Heather, she and Amanda shared many secrets. Their relationship was so strong that Amy had asked Amanda to be a junior bridesmaid in her wedding.

"Amanda, I have a basket filled with items that signify the things I've learned and shared with you.

"There is a phone to remind you of all the late night and early morning talks that we had and secrets that we shared. The bunny signifies all the smiles and hugs that you have given me that brightened my days. A heart to symbolize how much you are loved and how you will never be forgotten. And an apple because everything I've learned about being a great teacher is because of you."

There were statements from both Heather and Amy that stuck out in my mind that made me smile. Each spoke of the conversations they had with her. It was nice to know that I wasn't the only one who had been having these unspoken conversations with Amanda.

Amanda's aunt Cia got up to speak with her family in tow. Her husband was holding their two-year-old daughter, and her barely five-year-old son Caden, was by her side.

She had only gotten a few words out when Caden started pulling at her arm to get her attention. When that didn't work, he did what most kids would do.

"Mom, Mom, Mom," he said, reminiscent of my favorite scene from the *Lion King*, when Simba is trying desperately to get his dad's attention. "Let me show everyone the picture I drew for Amanda."

His mother could never resist his smile. She assumed he would just hold up his 'masterpiece' for everyone to see so she said okay. Caden had other ideas and grabbed the microphone out of her hand.

"Hi, everyone. My name is Caden. I drew a picture for Amanda and want to tell you about it."

He held the paper in his left hand as he pointed to the objects in his work of art with the microphone so that everyone could see. "It has a big sun and rainbow in the sky. The rainbow has all kinds of colors in it. That's why they call it a rainbow.

"I drew a picture of aunt Jen's house. It has a chimney with smoke coming out of it. See—it's right here," explained Caden, pointing to the curls of smoke.

"Over here is my mom," he said touching the stick figure of an adult.

"But this is what is so much fun about coming to see Amanda. She has a wheelchair."

His little eyes were smiling as he pointed to the other side of the picture. He was so proud when he said, "This is me pushing her in her wheelchair. I like coming to see her and playing with all of my cousins."

The crowd laughed at the playfulness of this little boy as he added, "That's all I wanted to say."

And just as quickly as he had grabbed it from her hands, he handed the microphone back to his mom.

"That's my son," said Marcia with a chuckle. "That boy's never at a loss for words."

She bent down and gave him a kiss on the cheek.

"Now, let's help your baby sister light the candle, shall we?"

Several more notes were shared from friends, family, and former respite workers who weren't able to attend, but who wanted to let Amanda know what she meant to them. One note thanked her for the lessons about life that came from working with her. Another shared how her time with Amanda had encouraged her in her goal of becoming a special education teacher.

Paul's sister Van had written a poem from the Canadian side of the family. She had taken the feedback that she had gotten from aunts, uncles, and cousins and made it into a poem.

Amanda's great-aunt Becky read well wishes and memories she had collected from the Baton Rouge clan. The most poignant of those statements was how Amanda had taught the family that every life is precious. Everyone has something to learn and teach.

It was the teaching about life that Amanda did so well. Mavis was a family friend who, along with her two kids, had lived with Jennifer and Paul for a brief time. As she got up to speak, I was reminded not only of Amanda's affect on people, but the hearts of gold that my daughter and son-in-law had.

Mavis and her children had hit an extremely rough patch in life. She was struggling with living in an abusive relationship and knew that she should file for a divorce, but hated the idea of giving up on her marriage.

I wish I could say I was as good as my daughters, but the truth is that I only planted the seeds of what being a good person looks like. They, on the other hand, took being there for others to a completely new level.

Mavis had commented to me in the past that she couldn't comprehend how the then family of five could open not only their hearts, but their home so willingly. Her words have always stuck in my mind, when she said, "They took us in without ever batting an eye. They just opened the door and gave us not just a place to live, but a home as well."

As she took her turn at the podium, it looked for a minute like she wasn't going to be able to get the words she wanted to say out of her mouth. But then Amanda flashed her a smile and it was obvious she was saying, *"You go, girl. You've got this. I've got your back."*

And with that smile, Mavis started to speak. "Amanda, I am so blessed by what your family did for me and my kids, but in all honesty, you were my saving grace.

"When I came to live with your family, my days were initially filled with darkness. There were times when I didn't know if I could get out of bed, and to be honest, most of those days, I really didn't want to.

"But God has a way of sending us what we need when we need it most. He doesn't just snap His fingers and make it all better. Instead, He often sends us an angel to guide our paths.

"Amanda, you were my angel. You were the gift from God that I so badly needed. Every time I saw you, you greeted me with a smile. You were a constant reminder that I could get up and make it through another day, because that is what you do.

"Others may not understand, but you were the underlying hope in every situation. Every frown and every tear I cried was met with a smile. Without realizing it, it became something I looked forward to and often leaned on to get me through the day.

"You were there with encouragement in your eyes. You were the reminder that no matter what happens and how someone may hurt you, they can't take your JOY and they definitely can't take your SMILE!"

Amanda displayed her signature smile as Mavis lit the next candle. She loved being there for others, but never fully realized the effect she had on those she interacted with.

In many ways, you could tell that Amanda was stunned by all the wonderful things people were saying about her. She understood her restrictions, but just like everyone else, she took pride in knowing that she could be there for others despite her limitations.

• • •

There was one testimonial that was different from all of the others. Up until that point, everyone had been telling Amanda what she meant to them. Paul Bohman, a family friend from West Virginia had sent a very different message for Amanda. It was the dream that he wished for her. A dream that everyone in the room had imagined at one point in time.

His words were read by Jennifer's friend Robbie.

"Amanda — Although you cannot communicate all of your ideas and emotions with words and may not be able to express love for people through touch, you have been successful in expressing yourself through small gestures and at times, huge emotional outbursts ☺

You are a beautiful young lady trapped in a body with limitations none can fathom.

Yet you are writing a novel of love deep within your mind, a novel filled with laughter and pain. In this novel, you are a little girl running through the fields chasing, butterflies.

You are a little girl who scrapes her knee as she climbs a tree. You sing songs and joke around with friends. You get mischievous and blame your brothers for things you did.

You are a young lady who has a crush on a boy in Sunday school and sneaks her first kiss.

I am sure your novel will be a masterpiece, and one day we will all enjoy reading it together. Until then, keep writing in your book. Fill it with your imagination and love, so that someday we can laugh and cry together."

Paul's words put a lump in every throat and a tear in every eye. There wasn't anyone in the room who hadn't fantasized about seeing Amanda walking or dancing at some point. There wasn't anyone who didn't wish for a miracle. That somehow she would start talking and never stop because she had so many years to catch up on.

But it was Paul Bohman's words that planted a seed in my brain that day. I knew the odds of a miracle were beyond astronomical. As much as I would have given anything to see my granddaughter dance and sing, I knew it was never going to happen.

However, what I could do was allow myself to be used as the vehicle to write that novel for her. To find a way to share her innermost thoughts, but more importantly, to give her a voice.

It was many years before that seed started to germinate and grow, but Amanda's words and the story of her life would finally make it to paper.

Chapter 16

The candle-lighting ceremony ended with tributes from Jennifer and Paul to their daughter. No one could mistake the love these three shared.

Paul went first. Not sure how I hadn't noticed it earlier, but at some point during the festivities, a small amplifier and guitar had been set up in the back of the room. Instead of heading to the front of the room when it was his turn to speak, Paul walked to the back and picked up the guitar.

It's funny how you can know someone for years, but not know they have a talent. My son-in-law definitely surprised me that day. He had written a song for Amanda and would play the guitar as he sang it. It may not have been a Grammy award-winning song, but there isn't a young girl out there who wouldn't be honored if her father wrote a song for her.

Paul had written the melody as well as the lyric and titled his song, *A Lifetime of the Good*. The words told the story of how Amanda came into their lives. It mentions a horror that no one could have imagined. Without going into details, he sang of how someone did their best to give her 'a lifetime of the bad.'

He brought to life in song how she refused to concentrate on the negatives of life. He sang how she brought happiness into their home and taught everyone to love no matter what the circumstance. For Paul, the final stanza of the song reflected what she brought to their family –

"Amanda gives us A lifetime of the good."

When he finished he started moving to the front of the room. But before he lit his candle, he stopped to give Amanda a hug, and knowing how much she loved it when he signed her name, he quickly spelled it out. After he kissed her on the cheek, he said, "I love you, my beautiful daughter."

• • •

Last, but not least, it was Jennifer's turn to let Amanda know what was in her heart. She knew she was the only thing standing between the sea of friends and dinner. She would make her comments brief, but she wanted her chance to let the crowd know how Amanda had enriched her life.

The testaments of the prior candle lighters had taken their toll. Jennifer had no idea what any of the guests were going to say. She had not given any instructions on the format for anyone's tribute. She had just asked that they speak from their hearts.

Hearing the words of others, the poems that had been written and the impact that Amanda had on people had left Jennifer's emotions raw. Speaking wasn't going to be easy, but as she looked into Amanda's smiling eyes, she found the courage to deliver the speech she had prepared.

"Thank you everyone for being here today to celebrate Amanda's birthday with us. I'll keep this brief so that we can get on with the festivities and have this lovely dinner that so many have helped us prepare."

She paused and looked lovingly at her daughter. The lump forming in her throat was similar to what many of us get when we are about to pour out our thoughts and feelings.

"Amanda, as you can tell by everyone's stories and letters so far, you touch lives without ever saying a word. Many have prayed that you will one day speak, but to say that you don't speak is like saying that God is not real because you have never heard His audible voice.

"Shortly after your injuries, the Family Resource Network was formed. It was a way for a small community in West Virginia to bring families and agencies together. You were the inspiration and I was asked to serve on the committee because of you.

"Two years ago, a lady named Terri Schiavo was in a nursing home. Some people said her life was meaningless because she could not speak, was fed by a tube, and could not walk. Because of you, we were able to go to Florida and meet her family. We saw firsthand that Terri brought her family joy—just as you do ours.

"You have to be the strongest little girl I have ever known. You fought so hard for your life. You have given me reason to fight for righteousness. I hope that everyone here will remember that God gives life and that no life is insignificant."

She walked over and gave Amanda a hug. The love between mother and daughter was a sight to behold.

"And Amanda, I'm working on a present for you, but it won't be ready until sometime in July."

Amanda looked puzzled. She couldn't imagine what her mom was talking about.

"Remember that little sister that you always wanted? Well, she will be here this summer."

The smile on Amanda's face was bigger than I had ever seen it and the whole room was suddenly buzzing with excitement. It was the perfect gift for Amanda. She would finally have the baby sister she so often dreamed of having. And just as Jennifer promised, Amanda welcomed her baby sister, Adison, in July.

After Jennifer lit the final candle, she turned back to the crowd. "Thank you all for sharing this day with us. Jeremy, if you will do the honors of saying the blessing over the food, we can let all these wonderful people eat. Enjoy everyone! We will cut the cake after dinner."

Chapter 17

After Amanda's party, life went back to the daily grind. Babies were born, birthdays were celebrated, and holidays came and went. In between it all, there were hundreds of baseball games to fill any void in time that this family might have had.

To say that life with two children with so many needs has its challenges is an understatement. But as time moved forward, this tightly knit family developed a rhythm to their routines. They included both Amanda and Rodney in everything they did.

But Jennifer wanted to give them their own unique experiences as well. With the severity of issues that both children had, the standard fare of activities—hiking, biking, skiing, cycling—wouldn't do. However, Jennifer worked tirelessly to find alternatives. She was successful in finding day camps in their area occasionally, but they were few and far between.

However, in 2007, when she was scouring the internet for possibilities, Jennifer came across a weeklong camp for individuals with all levels of special needs. Participants had to be ten years or older and were paired with a volunteer buddy for a week. She called me one day barely able to contain the excitement of what she had found.

"Mom, you aren't going to believe what I found for Amanda and Rodney! You know how I'm constantly looking for things for them to do. Well, I found a five-day overnight camp for special needs kids. I'm surprised I've never seen this before, but it is called Camp 4:13. It is run by the Assembly of God organization and is staffed with volunteers who come in from around the country.

"You're never going to believe where it is. Go ahead, take a wild guess."

"Really? You know how bad I am about guessing. It will be much easier if you just tell me when and where it is."

She wasn't going to let the guessing part of the conversation be over.

"When Marcia and I were kids, what was our favorite place to visit?"

"Well that's not a hard question. You loved visiting Gramps and Grandma. Is it in Arkansas?" I asked.

"You guessed it. And not only is it in Arkansas, but it is ten miles from the front gates to the Village."

I could tell she was getting nostalgic. She had loved going to Arkansas when she was younger and then as an adult with her own family.

"You know, I never thought of us as being poor growing up. I guess since all of our 'vacations' when we were younger were centered around those yearly trips maybe we were. But we were rich in so many other ways.

"Being with your dad and Grandma was the best. I loved how he used to take us fishing and to the park. And he was so excited when we would help him grill burgers." Her voice was letting me know that the memories were getting to her.

"Grandma taught us her secrets for making the best cakes, cookies, and desserts. But I think our favorites were riding in the golf cart and our yearly trip to the local rock shop.

"I know we spent time with them when they lived in Texas, but all my memories have morphed into our time spent in Arkansas. Watching the kids enjoying those same things makes me smile. They look forward to these yearly trips as much as Marcia and I did.

"I don't remember what year your dad and Grandma Betty moved there. Do you?"

"Believe it or not, it was March of 1983. I remember so many times putting you girls on a plane to spend a couple of weeks with them. Even after my dad died in 1988, neither you, nor your sister, nor Betty were willing to give up that time together.

"I think this was the beginning of our FOO vs FOC theory."

She laughed. "You know Mom, that last acronym raises eyebrows every time you say it."

"Yes," I said, laughing. "Which is why I always try to explain it within seconds of saying it. Reality is that each of us has both a Family of Origin—our FOO—and a Family of Choice—our FOC.

"If we are lucky the two coexist peacefully. Unfortunately, our FOO is often wrought with emotions and baggage that make them harder to navigate. Our FOC steps in when we don't have strong ties to our biological origins, or when we live too far away and we don't have that day-to-day interaction.

"I'm so proud of how you created your own family of choice with Amanda and Rodney, along with a whole list of friends who support you on a daily basis. There is always room in our hearts to love others." Now I was getting overwhelmed.

"I think of how when my dad died, I was so sad because he wasn't going to get to see you and your sister turn into such magnificent people. But then when Betty met Bob, we were complete again."

"Yes, I know exactly what you mean. Grandpa Bob is so much like Gramps. The way he loves all of these little rug rats warms my heart. He accepted us, but more importantly, he loved us just the way Grandma did from the first time we met him."

"Yes he did. It was as if I never lost my dad once he was a part of our lives. He and I had such great talks when we would visit. I think his pride in you girls was what filled in that gap from my dad.

"Yeah, Mom, I know exactly what you mean. Our FOO and FOC definitely show how lucky we are. It's what you taught both Marcia and me. There is no greater gift than love."

Her thoughts shifted back to the conversation regarding camp. "We would need to change our yearly visit with Grandma and Grandpa Bob from the Fourth of July week to the first week in August. Do you think that would be a problem for either them or Marcia?"

"I don't see why it would be. Give your sister and me the dates. I'm sure we can adjust our schedules. We are still months out so I don't see a problem with having our visit coincide with camp. I'll let your grandmother know and make sure it works for her and Bob. But I can't see why it would be a problem to change the dates."

"Mom, you aren't going to believe this camp. Each attendee has a designated buddy who stays with them the entire time. They will feed them and give them their meds, but more than that, the activities are amazing. They will take them swimming and riding in go-carts. They have arts and crafts activities, movie nights, and sing-alongs."

Her enthusiasm was now bubbling over. "Have no idea how long it has been in existence, or why it is just now coming up in my searches, but now I know what to tell you to get both Amanda and Rodney for their birthdays this year. A donation to help with the cost would be great. It's not as expensive as you might think. I'm sure the fact that it is staffed by volunteers from around the country is the reason it is so affordable."

• • •

Amanda's excitement about camp could never be contained as we started the preparations for our yearly Arkansas vacation. She enjoyed the freedom of being on her own so to speak. She would often see many of the same participants and volunteers each year. And Amanda was a crowd favorite. Jennifer would get reports from her caregiver at the end of camp, and Amanda was always animated when she was picked up on the last day.

"Granny, I can't believe it has already been five days. It seems like we just got here. I had so much fun. We saw some really funny movies. My favorite was Marley and Me. *That little pup reminded me of aunt Cia's dog Sydney. Swimming was fun too, but my favorite was the go-carts. I'm ready for next year!!!"*

She was so happy to be a part of something that was all about her.

"And Granny, guess what?" She was reminding me of her Mom and wanted me to play a guessing game.

"Look in my bag." She was grinning from ear to ear.

"What's this? You got the ribbon for favorite camper again!!" I gave her a huge hug.

"You know you are always my favorite. How many years does that make now?" The smile on my face was as big as hers.

"Yes I did!! It makes me feel so good to be given this award. I don't think I do anything that is so special, but everyone says it's my smile." She cocked her head to flash her winning look.

"Yes, missy, it is definitely your smile. You may not be able to have conversations like everyone else, but you speak volumes with those eyes of yours. Not to mention how your smile can melt even the hardest of hearts."

"Granny, you have to say that," she responded, rolling her eyes as only girls her age could do.

"But you know it is true. You touch people in a way that all of us wish we could. You remind each of us how important life is. And that is a gift which can't be denied. That is why you keep winning the favorite camper award."

"I don't do anything special. It's just me being me."

Her modesty was refreshing. She truly didn't see that what she did was special. She took her gift in stride and shared it freely with everyone. That is what made her so unique.

Chapter 18

One of the greatest lessons we can all learn about life is that change is inevitable. My grandmother taught me that, and one of my missions in my relationship with my grandkids is to pass that lesson on.

Amanda had dealt with a lot of change during her lifetime and her resilience never ceased to amaze me. In 2009, there was one more opportunity to embrace a new chapter.

"Granny, are you ready for the invasion and the takeover of your house?" She was smiling because she knew it was going to be an adjustment, but knew how much I loved having all of them around.

I had to laugh as I said, "I'm not really sure. You guys come with a lot of stuff."

"Can you believe that of all the places Dad could have chosen to do his sabbatical, he ended up at Rice University? Do you think this big house can handle seven more people? Do you think you can handle it?" She laughed, but already knew the answer. I was thrilled to have the opportunity to spend more time with them.

"I'm not sure." I was now laughing. "You guys have a lot of stuff. I think you brought everything, but the kitchen sink with you."

"I'm kind of sad to be leaving all of my friends, but I'm looking at this as a new adventure. Now we will be in the same city with you, aunt Cia, Caden, and Bryce. It's going to be fun. Plus it will make holiday and birthday celebrations a lot easier."

I loved the pragmatic side of her. Things would be different, but she never failed to find the silver lining.

As they settled in to a 'new norm,' Amanda was enjoying her new school. Jennifer was extremely pleased with the curriculum that the school offered for special needs teenagers. Her battles with previous schools had left her in tears way too many times.

All of the grandkids were enjoying the opportunity that being in the same town afforded them. But time has a way of slipping by so quickly. It felt as if they had just arrived when I found myself having another conversation with Amanda. A full school year had passed.

"Granny, I'm really going to miss living here with you. I can't believe school is ending in a couple of weeks. I miss my friends in Natchitoches, but I've made so many new friends here. Part of me doesn't know if I want to go back."

"I know exactly what you mean. But we still have a couple of months together. Our Arkansas vacation is coming up which means you get to go to Camp 4:13 again." That thought seemed to make her happy.

It was less than a week after that conversation that Paul got some very unsettling news. We often think of our higher education system being more stable than most jobs, but in a climate of dramatic cutbacks and fiscal challenges, universities are not exempt. It came as a huge shock to the family when Paul was told that his department at Northwestern State University was being dismantled. This is not what you want to hear when you have a family to provide for.

He would have to go back for one year, but after that, he would have to take a catastrophic cut in pay or find a new job. Fortunately, he found a new job right before Christmas in 2010.

"Granny, can you believe we are moving to Texas? And not just anywhere in Texas. We are moving back to League City!"

I loved seeing her so excited.

"I was wondering where we might end up. It was scary at first. Mom and Dad were talking about places we could go. There was a university in Arkansas not far from Grandma Betty. And I even heard them discuss the possibility of moving back to West Virginia.

"It is beautiful there, but is it wrong that I wouldn't have wanted to go back? Too many bad memories from that place. But I would have made the best of it if that's what they wanted to do."

"I can imagine that could have been hard for you. But we don't have to worry about that now. I can't believe that I'm going to have all of my family together in the same city now permanently! How did I ever get so lucky?"

She gave me a smile as she said, *"I just used my magic powers. Bet you didn't know I had them."*

"I'm not surprised at all. Your life is one big miracle. You have shown me over and over again that there isn't anything you can't do."

I was certainly glad that she had used one of those miracles to get the family to Texas. Her new life consisted of making friends at yet another new school as the house they bought was in a different school district. She made the transition easily and quickly acclimated to her new routine.

She was developing close ties with a new group of respite workers. Since the beginning, she had developed very strong friendships with those who helped care for her. It wasn't unusual for these women to stop by and say hello even when they weren't working.

The other big change was that her brother was now playing for a homeschool baseball team—the Eagles. Amanda became a fixture at all of Justin's games. It was always a thrill for her when a member of either the Eagles or the opposing team would come by to say hello before the game. For Amanda, cheering her brother on had become one of her greatest joys.

Chapter 19

Since Amanda seemed to be able to find beauty in almost everything that she did, I was surprised when I saw sadness on her face one day. It was our last day of vacation in Arkansas in August of 2015. Amanda had just returned from camp, but her normal excitement had been stolen by the news she had just heard. The look on her face was one I had never seen before.

As I made my way over to the couch to sit with her, the sadness that filled her eyes broke my heart. "Hi, my sweet girl. What's wrong? Are you okay?"

"Oh Granny, have you heard the news?" she asked.

I could see the tears forming in her eyes, and realized it must be the message we had received about Nathan.

"Sweetie, are you talking about Nathan?" assuming she had overheard her mom talking to Michelle. How do you tell someone that her very first friend has died?

"Yes, Mom told me. I just can't believe it. He was way too young. I can't imagine how Michelle is feeling.

"Granny, how can this be happening? He was barely nineteen-years-old. How could he be..." She stopped not wanting to say the word.

"I know it is hard to understand, but sometimes these things just happen. Death is not something any of us will escape."

"Granny, what does it mean to die? I've heard Mom and Dad say that I have cheated death so many times. That I'm a fighter and always have been. But I'm not sure if I know what that means sometimes."

I had thought that the most challenging talk a parent would have with their child was about the birds and the bees. Trying to explain death is a lot harder. Wasn't sure how I could delve into the complexity of death when I barely understood it myself.

"I know it is hard to comprehend. Death is not something any of us likes to think about. And what your mom and dad mean when they say you are a fighter is that you have overcome so many obstacles even when the doctors thought you wouldn't make it. You have fought long and hard to live despite the odds.

"But sometimes things happen, and as difficult as it is, we have to accept that our moving on is all part of a bigger plan."

"Granny, what does it mean to die?" she asked again.

My first thought was *Holy crap. She isn't going to let this go.* I knew she had been to a few funerals in her day, but not of anyone who meant as much to her as Nathan had. But if truth be told, I had no answer. He was her first friend and that little boy had made her feel normal. Their move from West Virginia meant that they rarely saw each other after that, but he would always hold a very distinct place in her heart.

"Amanda, death means that our bodies no longer function. Sometimes there are accidents. Just like the one Nathan was in.

"Sometimes people are killed in wars, and other times people are so sad they make the decision to end their own life. But most of the time, people die from old age. Our bodies aren't meant to last forever and at some point they just give out."

Didn't know if I should keep trying to explain it, but she was looking at me so intently, that I decided to continue with my thoughts. "However, death is often seen as a little more complicated than just our bodies ceasing to exist. Everyone has their own opinion of what happens when we die."

I could tell she was trying to process what I was saying, but was afraid that my answers weren't satisfying her or that I was giving her too much information.

"But what actually happens when we die?" She wasn't going to let the question go until she understood.

I was wishing I could call her mom over and have her continue our talk, but then I would have to try and explain these unspoken conversations that I had with her. And I wasn't sure how I could describe them so that they made any sense.

"Okay, I can only tell you what it means from my perspective, but just know that other people have their own ideas and belief systems."

"I understand," she said. *"I'm just curious as to what happened to Nathan now that he is dead."*

"For many of us, we think that our bodies are just vessels to hold our souls. When we die, our bodies cease to exist, but our souls live on. That is the basis of what you have been taught all of these years in your Sunday school classes and in the sermons that you have heard in church."

"Yep, I have heard that many times. Do you think Nathan is in heaven? Will I see him if I die? Will I be able to see you, my mom and dad, and my brothers and sister? What about aunt Cia, Caden, and Bryce?

"Do you think Nathan and I will be able to go do all the things I've never gotten a chance to do if I die? Will my body be whole again? Will I be able to run around and dance? Will I be able to eat Thanksgiving dinner? Will I be able to...?"

"Slow down," I said, smiling at the onslaught of questions . 'You are asking a lot of questions, and I don't have the answer to any of them. But the truth of the matter is that none of us knows what happens when we die. It's a personal faith and belief system that each of us has.

"I can only speak for myself, but yes, I do think there is an afterlife. But what that looks and feels like is different from what others may think. Our beliefs about what happens after we die are very personal to each of us.

"But I have to admit, in my perfect scenario, I do see you doing all of the things that you didn't get to do while you were here."

I stroked her arm and she gave me a big smile. *"Granny, a lot of what you say is similar to the conversations I've had with Dad about dying. Does it seem odd that I'm not afraid to die?"*

That was not what I expected her to say. But maybe the number of times she had come so close to death brought her a comfort that I didn't comprehend. Maybe her conversations with her dad about life and death had more of an influence then he realized.

"Amanda, when you first came into our lives, the doctors weren't sure if you would make it two years. But now look at you—you are twenty-four years old. You have defied all the odds. You have made our lives so full, and you help people see the good in life and help them cope with the bad. That's something few people have the ability to do.

"Don't worry about Nathan. It may seem strange, but I believe that we don't leave this earth until the job that we were sent here to do is done. And if that is the case, then Nathan was needed in heaven. Just know that he will be the first person to greet you at the Pearly Gates as they say."

"It's nice to know he will be waiting for me. I'm not going to worry about death or dying anymore."

I was glad to know my conversation had helped her. She seemed at peace with Nathan's death, which was what I hoped to accomplish.

The smile returned to her face. Our talk had eased her mind. Everything was going to be okay.

Chapter 20

Six months later, that conversation came crashing in on me. Things were about to change again.

As most of us look back on our lives, sometimes a series of events seem more like a dream than they do reality. But in the light of day, we are faced with knowing that what we just went through was real. The moments that play out are forever a part of who we are.

Sometimes those events are reminiscent of a dream. They leave us wondering if they really happened. Sometimes that dreamlike state is more of a nightmare. And for five days in that first week of February 2016, the chain of events that were about to unfold found me in a situation I had no skillset to handle.

My job gave me the luxury of only having to go into the office once a week. So on that first Monday in February, I was doing what I normally do. The alarm had been set for a 4:15 am wake up call. That always seemed terribly early, but my reasoning was twofold: first, so that I could beat the traffic and second, to make it to my desk for a 6:30 am meeting.

That morning was a carbon copy of every other Monday except for one thing. While I was drying my hair, something made me go get my phone. I don't recall a time of ever looking at it until I was heading out the door. But there is something inside each of us that can't be explained.

Some call it intuition, others would say it's psychic. Some say it is a connection we have with our loved ones and friends. It's that invisible thread that links us together. A cosmic force that makes us stronger as a team when we are weak as individuals. That inner strength which we tap into and is fortified by the ties that join us.

As I looked at my phone, I was surprised to see two text messages from Jennifer to Marcia and me.

The first message read, "Paul took Amanda to the ER around 12:30 am. Call me when you get this message." For a split second, I felt a huge wave of panic come over me. Then I read the second message. "Things got really scary around 1:15 am...she is stable now...no need to call."

I wasn't sure what I should do. If I called, I was sure to wake Jennifer up. Best course of action at that time was to keep getting ready and head to the office.

As the time was getting closer to leave the house, my mind kept going back and forth. But then I realized that I didn't want to make the 50.4 mile trip to the office, to only have to turn around one or two hours later and head to the hospital.

I couldn't envision that the outcome wouldn't be the same as the last few times Amanda had to be hospitalized. Almost every year for the previous three years, Amanda would get very sick and end up in the hospital for a few days right after the first of the year.

Her spirit was intact, yet it was obvious that her body was weakening. But she had been a fighter since that fall night in 1994. Multiple times her body failed her and the doctors thought she wasn't going to make it. Each time she fought back, even when there was a DNR in place. There was no reason to think this time was going to be any different.

I decided to turn on my computer so that I could ping my co-worker in The Hague to let him know what I was doing.

"Good Morning, Jasper ☺. Yes I can actually say that since it's one of the few times I'm online before it's noon there."

He responded immediately with, "Hey boss. Yes, it's not even 11 yet. Anything wrong? Aren't you normally driving in at this time of day?" was the message I got back.

"I was going to go into the office, but then I got a text from Jennifer. She said Amanda is in the hospital. I think I'm going to stick close to home today. A little worried I may need to go up there or Jennifer might need me to help with the other kids. I'll just take the few meetings I have from home and see what happens."

"Sounds like a plan. Let me know how things are going. I know there isn't much I can do from 5,000 miles away, but I'll let the others know to keep all of you in their thoughts."

I can't imagine what my father would think with all the texting that goes on these days. I'm sure that to his generation, it would seem peculiar as their world was centered around face-to-face human interaction. Ours is short text messages, posts on

Facebook, Twitter, Instagram, or Snapchat to let others know what is going on.

I continued to answer emails and looked at my calendar for the day. It had fewer meetings than normal, and my week was oddly clear when I checked my schedule. It's almost as if the universe knew weeks in advance that my attention would need to be elsewhere.

I kept debating with myself as to when to call Jennifer. I didn't want to wake her up, but since it was close to the time to get Rodney on the bus, I decided it was safe to call.

"Hi, sweetie. I saw your text a little earlier. Why didn't you call the house?"

"Hi, Mom. I would have if things had gotten worse. Was waiting to hear from Paul and then I was going to send out another message," she replied

"You still should have called," I said, trying to get the right mix of sympathy and irritation in my voice. What is it about all of us that we 'hate to bother' someone? Especially when a sickness is involved.

"I know, I know. But we were just waiting to see how things were going. She seems to be doing better for now except for the elevated heart rate. The doctor should come in around 9 this morning to see her and give us the results of some of the tests," Jennifer explained. But knowing her as I did, I could tell she was trying to hide her fear.

"What hospital is she in? Are you going up there after you put Rodney on the bus?" I asked.

"No, I'm going to take Joseph and Adison to their Classical Conversation class and then head up to the hospital. She's at Clear Lake Medical. The new heart wing across from the main hospital," was her reply.

"Okay, I'll meet you there around 8:30," hoping that my voice was remaining calm.

"It's not necessary," she said. "Paul is there. You don't need to come. I'll keep you posted on how things are going."

Her words fell on deaf ears. "No, I can take the day off and get you and Paul some food or drinks and help out with the kids."

Something told me it was going to be a long day and maybe an even longer night, but I didn't want her to know that.

Chapter 21

When I got to the hospital, it was obvious that things weren't going well. I was stunned by this turn of events because I had just seen Amanda three days earlier, and she was her normal cheerful self.

I knocked and then opened the door to see my son-in-law standing next to her bed, gently holding her hand. He smiled when he saw me and momentarily left her side to come give me a hug.

"Thanks for coming. But you really didn't have to. We would have let you know how she was doing. "But then he added, "I'm glad you are here."

He walked back to where he had been standing and softly touched Amanda's forehead.

"Amanda, Granny's here," was all he said.

As I walked over and took her hand, I was overcome with worry. We often can't see the elephant in the room as they say, but there was no not seeing it. Amanda was tethered to six separate machines, each one slowly dripping either an antibiotic, painkiller, or nourishment into her body.

Her blood pressure was slightly above normal, but the number that concerned me was her heart rate. I now understood what Jennifer meant when she had mentioned her elevated heart rate. It was fluctuating between 148 and 155 beats per minute. I knew from previous hospital visits with her that the norm was between 60 and 100. Her heart rate was much too fast.

Jennifer arrived a few minutes after I got there. She knew the doctor would be making his rounds soon and she wanted to hear what he had to say. We didn't have to wait long before there was a knock at the door.

"Good morning," the doctor said to Jennifer as he introduced himself and shook her hand as he had when he met Paul earlier. "I wish I had better news for the two of you, but her latest test results aren't looking good."

Jennifer and Paul were listening intently as he told them the outcome of the most recent tests. Unfortunately, everything was off the charts. My comprehension of the conversation was limited from a medical perspective. If I didn't know better I would have thought he was speaking a foreign language, but the part I did understand took my breath away.

"Mr. and Mrs. Withey," he said, "you have one very sick little girl."

Paul immediately responded, "Yes, but we have been here with her before. For the past few years, we have ended up in the hospital during the winter months."

Reality wasn't setting in, and I could see the pained expression on the doctor's face as he continued to fill them in on her condition. "That may be what has happened in the past, but, please forgive me, I have to be as honest with you as I can. I can't tell you exactly what happened, but my professional opinion from looking at her test results leads me to believe that at some point in the past two days, she must have aspirated some saliva.

"Most people don't realize it, but our saliva is probably the nastiest and most deadly thing on earth. I think it is what is causing the massive infection in her lungs."

Not to be intimidated by his words, Jennifer asked, "So what's our plan of action?"

Her years of experience with three of her five children having had major hospital stays was coming in handy. "This isn't our first rodeo with her, so please recognize that we aren't most parents. We want the full story, and either Paul or I will be here with her until she gets better."

To make sure she was getting her point across she added, "We are used to taking a very active role in her care."

I chuckled to myself—this doctor had met his match with these two. He had no idea how the years of taking care of special needs children had made them a formidable duo.

My interaction with the health care industry was much more limited. Maybe that is why I heard his next words so differently. And maybe by being an observer rather than the parent, my vision was slightly clearer at that moment.

"As I said, you have a very sick girl." He paused. Not to let them ask questions, but it was obvious that the next words were constricting in his throat. It wasn't the first time he had to deliver this kind of news to a family, but I could tell that no amount of practice ever made it any easier. He knew he had to be honest, but knew that these two individuals standing in front of him wanted nothing more than to hear that everything was eventually going to be okay.

"I wish I had a better prognosis for you, but with everything the way it is now…" He paused again. Although his eyes were watering, he kept his composure. "I'm sorry, but Amanda has less than a ten percent chance of surviving this."

The words hung over us like a dark cloud. Our breathing suddenly became labored as we were all letting the words sink in.

Paul was the first to respond. "She's beaten so many odds. This is just one more challenge for her." He put his arm around Jennifer and smiled as he looked at Amanda. "She's a fighter. She has been since we got her."

He turned his attention back to the doctor. "Just let us know when the next test results come in. We appreciate all that you are doing."

As their foreheads touched, I marveled at the strength that the two of them had. I never doubted that together, Jennifer and Paul, could get through anything.

At that moment, I was less than optimistic. This was the day I had been dreading and had somehow convinced myself would never happen. The natural order of things was for all of my children and grandchildren to survive me. Something told me that might no longer happen.

* * *

The three of us stood around for a while chatting, making small talk while encouraging Amanda to fight to get better. As it got close to lunchtime and since Paul hadn't eaten in a while, I suggested that the two of them go grab a bite to eat. I would sit with Amanda until they returned.

They were reluctant at first, but finally agreed to step away for a little bit. There was a cafeteria across the street in the main hospital, so they didn't have to get in their car to go anywhere.

They told Amanda that they would be back shortly and that Granny was staying with her. The smile that we would normally see wasn't there. You could tell she was tired and didn't have the energy to give even the faintest of smiles.

As they left the room, I walked over and stroked Amanda's arm. Fear had taken over my body, but there wasn't much I could do, but be there for her and the rest of the family. Eventually, I was going to need to tell others she was in the hospital, but knew that could wait.

There was a knock on the door and the respiratory technician walked in. "Hi, I'm Jake. I'm here to give Amanda a breathing treatment."

"Hi, Jake. I'm Gwyn, Amanda's grandmother. Her parents just stepped out to get a bite to eat. Do you need me to get them for you? They just left a few minutes ago, so I doubt if they have even made it to the cafeteria."

"No, this is just a routine treatment. Only takes about fifteen minutes. Nothing unusual about it," he answered.

"Is it okay if I stay?"

"Certainly. Let me know if you have any questions."

I sat there debating for what seemed like an eternity, but finally got up the courage to speak.

"Can I ask you something about her condition?" were the words I finally spoke. "The doctor was in here a little earlier. He said that her chances of surviving this are less than ten percent.

The words were harder to say than I ever imagined. "Do you think she is going to pull through?"

The look on his face told me what he thought, but I still wanted to hear the words. I wanted to know what we were facing. History had taught me that Amanda and the word 'miracle' were interchangeable.

He took a deep breath and said, "I'm not a doctor, so I'm not going to give you any medical advice or information." He took another deep breath. "I can only tell you how these things normally turn out from my years of experience."

His eyes searched mine as he tried to decide if he should go on. I nodded and he continued.

"I wish I could tell you otherwise, but in all the years I've been doing this, the numbers from the test that I'm seeing, along with her elevated heart rate over the last twelve hours, as well as the look in her eyes are telling me..." He stopped again, and it seemed he wondered if he should continue.

"Please go on. I know I've asked a very tough question, but it will help me help my daughter and son-in-law if I have more information."

"That's understandable and in your shoes, I would want the same thing. But this just isn't what I ever want to tell people. Miracles can happen. However, I can't recall a single time when I've seen similar circumstances where the patient pulled through. I'm so very sorry, but I doubt she will last another twenty-four hours." His chest heaved as the words came out.

I was speechless. There were no words left to say. No questions left to ask.

Chapter 22

Jennifer and Paul returned from lunch, so I told them I was going to go to the lobby area to make some calls. There were a few people I still needed to let know that Amanda was in the hospital.

Before I dialed a number, I sat there and closed my eyes. My mind drifted back to the conversation I had with Jennifer when she and Paul were deciding whether to take on the responsibility of the beautiful woman who was now fighting for her life. The memories were as if they took place yesterday, but the reality was that it was now twenty years later. Nevertheless, the conversation that let me know I was going to be a grandmother was still engrained in my being.

"Mom, I need your advice."

"Okay, sweetie, what's going on?"

"You know, Paul and I have been trying for years to get pregnant."

"Oh my gosh, are you telling me you're pregnant? How exciting! This is so fantastic. I'm so happy for you. When are you due? Have you seen a doctor yet?"

As I continued to ramble and gush over the news and ask twenty million questions, I didn't give her a chance to finish telling me the whole story.

"Mom, Mom, slow down. I'm not pregnant."

"What? I thought when you mentioned how you had been trying to have a baby, that you were pregnant. Okay, I'm confused. What do you need advice about? Are you going to a fertility specialist?"

"No, we are thinking of becoming foster parents."

Knowing the two of them, I wasn't surprised by the statement.

"I think that is fantastic! Infant? Toddler? Teenager? Boy or girl?"

Again, I was overwhelming her with questions without letting her answer. My heart swelled with pride as I envisioned Jennifer and Paul helping a child who was lost in the system.

"Mom, it's not quite that simple, which is why I wanted your advice. We want to take in a little girl with special needs."

I have to admit, I hoped my voice would hide my confusion and concern about what she was telling me. I needed to stay focused, but more importantly, the situation called for clarity. I was so proud of her and Paul from one perspective. Taking on the responsibility of someone with special needs is not something many people can or are willing to do.

I remember wondering how could I give her advice when my whole being wanted to protect her from what might lie ahead. Yet I knew that those with disabilities had always been her soft spot. Her work in high school and her initial major in college were all geared to special education.

On the other hand, being able to help special needs children versus taking one into your home is very different.

"Okay, so tell me about her. What kind of special needs does she have? And what do you need from me?"

I already knew that the decision was made and that no matter what I said, this almost four-year-old little girl called Amanda was about to become a part of our lives.

"Should we do this? Are we making the right decision?" she asked.

Being the practical person that I am, I told her what I needed to as well as what she wanted to hear.

"Jennifer, I know you have a big heart. And I know your faith has brought you to this moment. I only have two things to say.

"Promise me that if the day ever comes when it is no longer possible for you to care for her, you will do what is best for both her and your family. Understand that it is not a failure on your part if you need help to care for her.

"But more importantly, know that there is room in all of our hearts to love her."

"So you are okay with your first grandchild being a little different?"

"Who in this family isn't a **lot** different?" I laughed out loud.

"So true. So true. Only one question left. Do you want to be Grandma, or Grams, or Granny?"

"I guess since I have a cement pond in my back yard, I should be Granny." And then the theme song from *The Beverly Hillbillies* started playing in my head. I think it was days before I could ever get it out of my mind.

And now it was back, but this time it didn't make me smile. It was more of an annoyance, because I knew this was the moment I had been dreading ever since we had that conversation.

• • •

There were so many people to call, but I really didn't know what to say. I decided to be pragmatic and just stick to the facts. I didn't want to be Chicken Little and start yelling that 'the sky is falling.' At the same time, I knew this was more serious than the previous trips to the hospital.

When we are faced with a crisis, our default is to seek our comfort zone. For me, that was my friend Iris. She and her husband Steve had known Jennifer and Marcia since they were eight and five years old.

As I dialed her number, I closed my eyes and could do nothing but pray. I trusted that the higher power that I called God was in control. That whatever would lie ahead would be the right thing.

But I didn't know if there was enough strength in the world to get me through what I worried was about to happen.

"Hi, Iris," I said with as much strength as I could muster. There is no memory of what I said to her. Only the fear of knowing that it was the beginning of a very long week and the most challenging moments a mother would ever have to bear.

Chapter 23

It has always amazed me how the invisible grapevine works. By early afternoon, the few people who had been contacted had each told a few individuals who in turn told others.

A steady stream of fellow homeschool moms and their families were dropping by to check on Amanda. This close-knit group was about to have a mom live through every parent's worst nightmare. It was as if they hoped that by gathering en masse, they could somehow stop the inevitable.

By 6 pm, the waiting room was filled to capacity. Everyone was coming by to spend a few minutes with Amanda and to let her know that they were praying for her.

My youngest daughter, her fiancé, Harry, and her two kids, Caden and Bryce, were there. My sister Geri and my best friend Iris, along with my goddaughter Katie had gathered as well.

As was the almost daily routine, Justin was scheduled to play in a game that evening, and this baseball family took the love of the game to a whole new level. It was a small team and every player counted. It didn't take a second thought to decide that he should be with his team. Joseph, and Adison would go to the game with him, and Rodney would stay at home with his respite worker.

The game would be a great distraction for at least a little while for these three siblings. Reality was that there wasn't anything they could do, but sit and wait with the rest of us. Coach Andy and others would bring Justin, Joseph, and Adison to the hospital when the game was over.

It was comforting to have so many people there holding vigil. They would take turns going into the hospital room to be with Jennifer and Paul and also to let Amanda know that they were there for her. As the evening progressed, I think I knew where things were headed when the nurses stopped enforcing the 'only three visitors at a time' rule.

• • •

It's funny how thoughts pop into our heads. I was struck with the memory of when Jennifer and Paul made League City their permanent home. There was a part of Jennifer that was afraid she would never make friends like the ones she had had in both West Virginia and Louisiana. It was tough starting all over again. But now there was a room full of friends doing what they could to support the family.

Not only were there fellow homeschoolers, but there were friends from church. At around nine o'clock, the majority of the baseball team showed up with Justin, Joseph and Adison in tow.

Justin and his teammates were all excited because they had just won a big game. Justin was beaming with pride since he had received the game ball that night. He may have told me about the play he made to deserve the game ball, but like so many other things, my memories were replaced by the fear of the unknown.

What I do remember was that he was holding on to the ball as if it were a crutch. I could see the thoughts going through his head as I watched him walking around the room asking everyone to sign it. It wasn't something that I had ever seen someone on the team do, so thought it was odd.

"Granny, can you sign my game ball? Going to have everyone here sign it," he said. His voice was cracking as he added, "I'm going to give it to Amanda."

I wondered how much more my heart could take. My seventeen-year-old grandson was giving her the one thing that meant more to him than words could describe. He was a baseball player from the moment he started walking. Nothing meant more to him than being on the field.

His sisters and brothers had all earned the t-shirt with the saying *I Don't Have a Life — My Brother Plays Baseball*. But he was going to give his big sister the one thing that he cherished the most- the game ball he had just received.

As I watched him gather more signatures, I was reminded of a conversation he had with a friend that I had overheard several years earlier. The entire family was in Natchitoches over the Thanksgiving holiday. It was going to be our first time to see the over 300,000+ Christmas lights and one hundred plus lighted displays that lined the banks of the Cane River facing Front Street.

How the conversation started is not something I remember, but one of Justin's friends made the comment about Amanda being adopted. Justin knew that she was, but in his mind, that detail was negated by the fact that she was his sister. The thing I remember most is him angrily saying, "No, she isn't adopted. She's my sister!"

In his mind, she was his sister. Adoption was just a formality and didn't change the facts.

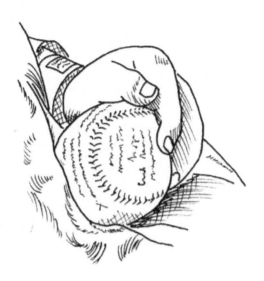

Chapter 24

Before the week began, I was under the misconception that the hardest thing a parent would ever have to endure was having one of their children die. But for me, I was now faced with something much worse. Watching my daughter's heart getting ripped to shreds and realizing I had no tools in my bag of mommy tricks to fix it left me powerless.

There were so many moments since I first set foot in Amanda's hospital room that didn't seem real. All too often, I felt my heart was in a vise, and some sadistic demon was getting great pleasure out of tightening the lever. I could see the look on the monster's face and hear his laugh as he tightened it to the point of breaking and then released it ever so slightly so that I could breathe again.

But as I stood there watching the tears flow down my daughter and son-in-law's faces trying desperately to hold on to hope, I was completely incapable of keeping the pain away that they would soon feel.

The nurse did her best to soften the harsh reality, but her words were daggers to their hearts. "Mr. and Mrs. Withey, I know you realize we are doing everything we can for Amanda, but I need to ask you a few questions in light of the results of the latest test."

Her voice was soft, but it couldn't mask the sadness. "I hate to bring this up, but we need to ask...." She paused as the words caught in her throat. "We need to know if you want to put a DNR in place."

My heart broke as I saw the looks on Jennifer and Paul's faces. They knew the question was coming, but it still didn't make it any easier. As Paul put his arms around Jennifer, her head rested on his shoulder. The tears were trickling down their faces as they clung to each other.

"I can't do it. I just can't do it," was all Paul would say.

"She's strong. She's a fighter. This can't be the end," Jennifer said through her tears.

The nurse had been standing there letting them have a moment to process what was happening. "I am so very sorry, and know we will do whatever you want, but unfortunately, we have reached the limit of what we can do to help her."

"Just give us a minute," Paul said. "We need to talk this over."

"Take all the time you need. Just let us know what we can do to help you" she said tenderly, and then quietly turned and walked out of the room.

Medical professionals deserve a great deal of respect for the often thankless job that they have. But the compassion in the nurse's eyes and the sadness in her voice told me that just as with the doctor, no matter how many times she had to deliver that kind of news to a family, it never got any easier.

• • •

At one point during the evening, a group of about fifteen people had gathered in Amanda's room. One was the pastor from the church they had attended for a while. He asked if he could pray for Amanda. Jennifer and Paul welcomed the gesture and all of us joined hands. His prayer was not only for her healing, but for acceptance of whatever the outcome.

Justin's teammates and their families were now taking turns coming into the room and saying hello. It was tough for these boys because the majority of them had probably never had to deal with the possibility of a death of someone so close to their own age. They were coming in to pay their respects to the young woman who had been a staple at their games for years.

At around 10 pm, Justin, Caden, and Katie were all in the room. They were the closest in age to Amanda and therefore had a lot more history with her than the younger grandkids.

All three of them were exhausted, but more importantly, they were grieving in a way that no teenager should have to. I marveled at their composure and the support they were showing one another, all of which were the result of the admiration they had for Amanda and a sign of how much she had influenced their lives.

My heart was filled with pride as I watched them stand together in support. I suggested they go wait with others where they could be a little more comfortable, but they refused, saying in unison, "We aren't leaving Amanda."

I briefly stepped away to go talk to some of the people who had gathered in support of the family. I was surprised that at such a late hour, the room was still filled with people. The nearly forty chairs were occupied by friends and family members. They weren't loud and boisterous. They were respectful of the two other families who were waiting on news of their loved ones as well.

But there was both sadness and joy in the room. Sadness for Jennifer and Paul. Sadness for all the siblings, cousins, aunts, uncles, and grandparents who were assembled. But there was joy at the thought of how Amanda had influenced everyone who was holding vigil for her. The outpouring of love was bigger than the room itself. People were there to support the family, but they were there because Amanda had touched each of their lives. They were grateful for the lessons she had taught them about the acceptance of individuals with disabilities.

Everyone knew that the family had been there since early that morning. Some brought snacks. Others brought blankets. Why are hospital areas always so cold?

Another friend brought toothbrushes and toothpaste. That's not something I would have ever thought about, but she knew we could be there for a long time and I was so taken by her gesture—and incredibly thankful.

When I returned to Amanda's room, I was taken aback by what I saw in the corner of the room. Justin and Katie were sitting next to each other in an oversized chair. Caden was perched across their laps. The three of them had their arms intertwined and had fallen asleep.

Although many of those holding vigil had left around midnight, several families stayed until after two in the morning. They didn't want to leave Jennifer and Paul, but many had to work the next day or get kids to school. Some just wanted to go home and get a few hours of sleep. What amazed me was that a number of people who left actually returned by 10 am the next morning.

I don't remember if I ever closed my eyes. I would think I would have, but mostly remember Joseph, Adison, and Bryce all taking turns and snuggling with me for a while. They may not have been aware of what they were doing, but their hugs were easing the sadness that surrounded me.

It was during that time as well that I recalled two recent memories of these children with Amanda. The first was of how Amanda loved it when Bryce and Adison were playing dolls. She could stare at them for hours as they created their own pretend world, but she loved it when they made her their real life doll. They loved playing with her long, wavy, light brown hair, and as they got older Bryce would teach Adison different types of braids. One time in particular, they created over twenty braids with Amanda's hair, and then braided the braids together until it was one big braid. They were so proud of the hairstyle makeover they had given her.

Joseph, on the other hand, was always about inclusion when it came to Amanda. Whether they were at a game, watching a movie, or a family activity, he made sure she was part of the action. Only ten days earlier, we had celebrated his tenth birthday. He had opted for a party at home so that Amanda could enjoy watching him turn to double digits.

They say that when we die, we see our lives flash in front of our eyes. That day, everyone in the room was seeing their life with Amanda through a different lens. They were recalling those special moments they had shared. Some were remembering holidays; others shared memories of birthdays, and some talked about sitting on my back porch holding her hand.

No one wanted to accept that we were nearing those final moments. But on Tuesday morning, Amanda's condition was worsening. As much as none of us wanted to admit defeat, we all knew it was time to let her go.

Jennifer and Paul could handle their good-byes. It was something they had accepted the moment they brought Amanda into their home. But acceptance and reality often don't mix—just like oil and water.

They knew that Justin would be going to college in a year and he was more capable of handling the situation. Rodney's disabilities left him completely unaware of what was happening. But how do you prepare a ten and nine year old for the loss of their older sister?

Joseph was the most sensitive of this brood. His level of empathy went well beyond his years. As he gave Amanda one last hug and kiss, tears were trickling down his face.

Adison, on the other hand, was losing her only sister. Amanda had loved her like only a sister could. She had sat and watched as Adison had played dolls with her and had tea parties. They had gotten their fingernails and toenails painted together. They had bonded over being the girls surrounded by three noisy brothers.

Marcia and her family stood together as they said their goodbyes. Caden had his arm around his mom as she stood next to the hospital bed and softly pushed Amanda's hair behind her ear. Bryce was touching her hand that wrapped around the game ball.

When it came time for my goodbye, I wasn't sure how I could do it. The only thing left was to have one last conversation with her.

"Hey, sweet girl," I said as I held her hand. "Granny is really going to miss you." I couldn't hold back the tears.

"Granny, don't cry. I need you to be strong because Mom and Dad are going to need you. I need you to tell them how much I love them.

"I'm ready to go run and play in the fields with Nathan. I will miss all of you, but I've accomplished what I was sent here to do."

"You've done that and more, my Manda Panda. Don't ever forget how much I love you."

As I kissed her cheek, my heart was breaking. I didn't want to leave, but I knew that Jennifer and Paul wanted to be alone with her as she took her last breath.

The kids and I all made our way to the waiting room. We would sit with the others until Jennifer and Paul came to tell us she was gone.

I was hoping against hope that there was one last miracle left in my sweet granddaughter, but unfortunately, that wasn't the case. It was a little after 11 am, when Jennifer and Paul walked into the waiting area. They didn't have to say anything. We all knew she was gone.

The twenty or more people who were there gathered in a circle holding hands. Paul asked all of us to bow our heads for a prayer. His words were simple, but filled with love.

"Thank you, Lord for the gift of Amanda. We knew she was only ours for a short time, but it doesn't make this any easier. She defied the odds over and over again. She was an inspiration to everyone who met her. She is now in heaven with you and no doubt already has her wings.

"Thank you for enriching all of our lives through her presence. For showing us what it means to be resilient and how important it is to be there for others.

"Amanda, we will all miss you. Amen."

Paul's words brought some comfort, but tears were flowing down every face. It had been twenty-eight hours since I had walked into the hospital. I had hoped against hope that Amanda was going to pull through.

I was overcome with grief. I assumed the hard part was over. But it was only beginning.

Chapter 25

As I said earlier, I think losing one of my daughters wouldn't be as painful as watching my child lose hers.

Before we left the hospital, I called the funeral home and made arrangements for them to come pick up Amanda's body. It took a while, but we finally headed back to their house. For the longest time we sat without talking. By late afternoon, people were stopping by and dropping off food. Several friends showed up to clean the house. And flowers were starting to be delivered.

I had done everything I could without Jennifer and Paul's help as it pertained to the funeral, but there were some things that would require their decisions. As much as I think they wished I could, they knew I couldn't plan Amanda's funeral without them.

Chaotic thoughts about life were going through my brain. I think it was a coping mechanism to not have to deal with the reality of eventually having to go to the funeral home. I was remembering the times when my daughters were little. How exasperating it was to give the constant reminders: "Eat your vegetables. Comb your hair. Brush your teeth. Feed the cat. Finish your homework." On Tuesday afternoon, I would have gladly given everything I owned to not have to give a reminder.

"Jennifer, we need to go to the funeral home." Those were the most painful words I've ever had to say to my daughter in my entire life.

"Mom, I just can't do it. Please don't make me go." Her eyes were still swollen from crying, and more tears were trickling down her cheek as she said the words.

"Sweetheart, I can't even imagine how trying this is for you, but it is something you and Paul and I need to do."

I was praying that someone would wake me and I would realize it was all just a bad dream.

"Can you please make the appointment? Just tell us what time we need to be there. And would you mind coming to pick us up and driving us there? I don't think either of us is capable at this moment in time."

Before she walked away, she gave me a hug, saying, "I'm going to go take a shower and get cleaned up. Would you mind getting the kids some dinner? There is plenty of food in the fridge."

I was reaching into the recesses of my brain to try and think of some words that would ease her pain, but my mind was as numb as hers. All I could think of was, "No problem. Take your time."

• • •

The strength of these two parents amazed me, but this was testing their resolve at a whole new level. As a family we had always been there for one another, but this was not something any of us was prepared for.

The words stuck in my throat, and all I could think of was that I didn't want to have to be 'the mom' at that point in time. I didn't want to have to be the one who took my daughter into a place that no parent ever wants to go. I wanted to turn back the clock to Monday morning before the chain of events that led us to this place started to unfold.

But you just can't stop being a mom when it isn't convenient. Every memory of my daughters putting their arms around my neck and kissing me on the cheek and saying 'I love you, Mommy' was flashing through my brain. Every memory of the pride that I felt as I watched them graduate from high school, college, get married, and bless me with seven grandchildren, was now being replaced with the one memory I hated more than I knew was possible.

Before I left to go home, I filled Jennifer in on the details of what we would do on Wednesday. "I'll pick you and Paul up around 1:30 tomorrow afternoon if that works for the two of you. Our appointment is at two o'clock. It shouldn't take us more than twenty minutes to get there, but who knows what traffic might be like. Does that work for you?" I asked knowing full well that nothing about this scenario worked for either of them.

"Yes, Mom, that works. Thanks for taking care of this for us."

• • •

The look of despair and sadness that was on their faces as we drove through the gates of Forest Park East Funeral Home and Cemetery was excruciating. They were about to have to make decisions that no parent should ever have to. Not only did they need to talk about the service itself, but also they would have to pick out a casket and decide on a burial plot.

For a few minutes, I wondered if they would get out of the car and go inside with me. Paul eventually opened his door, and said, "I guess there is no way we can put this off, is there?" He was making a statement and asking a question simultaneously.

"Unfortunately, there isn't," I said feeling like the most horrible person on the planet for making them do this. I would have done it for them, but this was their daughter, their first child. And as much as they hated it, it was the last thing they would ever have to do for her.

We were greeted by the receptionist who took us to a private room. There were reminders everywhere as to why we were there. Various plaques adorned the walls featuring different styles of markers available, along with granite samples. The minutes dragged on, and even though there wasn't a clock in the room, it was if I could hear the ticking of a clock marking each second. Although it seemed like an eternity, the funeral director, Marcus, walked in right on time. I have often wondered what makes someone choose a career in the business of dying. How can you go into the office every day knowing that you will be confronted with people who are dealing with one of the lowest points of their lives?

There was an obvious protocol to what needed to be done. First order of business was setting a date and time for the services and visitation. We had hoped to have the service on Saturday to allow more time for friends and family to travel, but unfortunately, there was no slot available.

It would have to be Friday or we would have to wait until the following week. They didn't think any of us could handle prolonging the inescapable reality of what we had to do, so Jennifer and Paul decided on Friday afternoon. We then set a time for the visitation on Thursday and discussed using the large chapel for the service itself. They would need to decide on music and the order of the service, but those were things they had time to think about.

Little did I know that deciding on dates and times was the easy part. The pain that comes with having to pick out a casket and final resting place was one hundred times worse.

Things had changed since the last time I had to help plan a funeral. The worst part of that experience had been walking through the room of caskets. Luckily, everything except choosing the burial plot was done through the 55-inch TV screen that was in the room. Somehow, it seemed a lot easier to do that than to be surrounded by the actual caskets.

With that decision made, it was time to make our way outside and into a waiting van. Marcus was going to show us several options for a final burial spot.

"Can we take a quick break before we go into the cemetery?" Jennifer asked. "I don't know if I can do this."

"It's okay, Jennifer," I said, then turned to Marcus and asked, "Can you give us a few minutes?"

"Of course, take your time. I have a couple things I need to do, so I'll go take care of some of the paperwork and give you all a few minutes."

I was told once by a prior boss to never apologize for something that is completely out of my control. But at the moment, I was devastated knowing that I had to make my daughter go through this process. Saying "I'm sorry" did not help the situation. She may have been forty-three years old, but my brave and courageous daughter was crying again. "Mom, why are we having to do this? Can you please wake me up from this nightmare? Surely this can't be happening."

"Jennifer, you know I would give anything if I could change all of this, but unfortunately, I can't.

"You are one of the strongest women I have ever known. And you and Paul gave Amanda such a wonderful life.

"We will honor her with this final tribute. Let's go see the options for a burial spot. It's the last thing on the list of what we have to do here today."

As they got up, Paul gave Jennifer a hug and then took her hand. We found Marcus and made our way to the van.

He showed us two mausoleums and several places on the property that were available. Most were rows deep in a specific section, and I wondered if we would ever be able to find the plot after Amanda was buried. One thing I learned before the end of the day was that just like in housing, the key to finding the right spot was location, location, location.

I felt we were getting nowhere when Marcus said, "There is one more spot that I can show you. It's a little more expensive than what we've just been looking at. Do you want to see it?"

"Why not?" I said. "It can't hurt to know all of our options."

As we drove to the farthest end of the cemetery on the right hand side of the property, Amanda's voice came into my head. It was the same sweet voice I had heard when we picked out her dress for her Sweet Sixteen party.

"Oh, Granny. It's perfect."

And it truly was. The plot was on the first row at the end of a cul-de-sac and was shaded by two gigantic oaks. There was a sidewalk along the side that said 'Handicap Ramp.' The irony of that was lost on none of us.

We didn't need to look any further. I didn't care if it cost twice as much as any other spot; I was at peace there and knew Amanda would be too.

Chapter 26

We went back to the office and signed all the papers. Marcus gave us a list of things to do—homework so to speak.

"That takes care of the majority of the items, but this is what I need from you by tomorrow afternoon. You can choose not to do some of it. We will make do with whatever you give us.

"First we need whatever outfit you want to have her buried in."

"How about her Sweet Sixteen dress?" I asked.

"I think she would like that, but it may not fit her anymore," Jennifer said.

"Then bring an alternative if you don't mind," Marcus replied. "We will do our best, but you are right, some things may not work."

I was wishing I had a piece of paper to make notes as he continued.

"Send me a file with pictures you want to have shown during the visitation tomorrow night and before the service on Friday. You can email them to me or if they aren't electronic copies, you can bring the actual photos to the office. We will be happy to scan them for you.

"I'll need the agenda you would like to follow for the service and any songs you want played. Here is my card with my phone number and email address. Please don't hesitate to call me if you have any questions."

As we got up to leave, it was a relief to know that most of the work was done.

Jennifer and Paul wanted to keep the service simple, so the decision was made that three of us would speak at her funeral. Amanda's Uncle Roland would go first. He was married to Paul's baby sister, Leanne, and had been designated as the spokesperson for the Canadian side of the family. I would follow Roland, and Paul would end the service with words from him and Jennifer.

It never crossed my mind that I wouldn't speak at her funeral. I had never been shy about speaking in front of crowds. I had taught classes through work. I had done speaking engagements at conferences and been part of keynote panels. None of those engagements or speaking at prior funerals had ever intimidated me. But being able to form a coherent sentence was suddenly an overwhelming thought.

Would I be able to say what I really wanted to say? Would I be able to convey to the people who were assembled to pay their final respects the meaning of Amanda's life? Would I start blubbering or make a complete idiot of myself by losing all self-control?

For the first time in my life, I was afraid of speaking in public. I went home right after dinner that night. I needed to collect my thoughts and knew that Jennifer and her sister could take care of getting pictures together. Paul would handle the other items. He would make the calls to people he and Jennifer wanted to be pallbearers, and he would get copies of the songs they wanted played.

Arrangements had been made for the family and friends who were coming from out of town. Carrie, Jennifer's best friend from high school was flying in from California. Paul and Beth would make the trek from West Virginia, and Cheryl and Roland would be coming in from Calgary. Other out-of-towners were luckily within driving distance and would not need to be picked up at one of the airports.

Everything was under control except for our emotions. And I wasn't sure when that control would kick in.

The next day, Paul delivered all of the items Marcus had asked for. Unfortunately, her Sweet Sixteen dress hadn't worked because she was so swollen from all of the medications she had been given in the hospital. Instead, she would be dressed in her favorite red shirt since red was her favorite color.

• • •

The visitation was another outpouring of love for the family. The room was filled with flowers and there was a steady stream of people coming in to pay their respects.

The slide show of pictures was a trip down memory lane. There were photos from when Jennifer and Paul first got Amanda. Snapshots of her holding all of her siblings when they were born. Reminders of camp and our Arkansas vacations. Pictures with many of her respite workers from over the years. Each image reinforced the power of her smile.

As the evening drew to a close, I was reflecting on two very different thoughts. The first was that with each death of a loved one or friend, we are given the opportunity to move forward with our lives with renewed purpose. We are reminded to not take a single day of our existence for granted. As a dear friend once told me, it's not about the number of days in a life, but about the life we put into our days. The second thought was about the kindness of others. Everyone who was there had a special place in their hearts for this grieving family. Not sure if they would ever know how much it meant to all of us to be surrounded by so much love.

Now all that was left was to go home and get a little bit of sleep. Friday was going to be a long day. It would be our final goodbye to a young woman who had changed all of us.

Chapter 27

Shortly after I got home, Roland and Cheryl arrived. I was thankful I wasn't going to be alone. Being single and living by myself has some advantages, but the night before Amanda's funeral was not one of those times when I wanted to be alone.

Roland and Cheryl were the designated representatives for the Canadian crew. Almost all of Paul's family lived in or near Calgary, and last minute flights were too costly for the entire family to fly in for the funeral. This clan consisted of ten brothers and sisters, so when combined with their respective spouses and children it would have totaled over forty plane tickets. As with many events of this significance, the group was comfortable with sending designated representatives when needed. It would often depend on work schedules, school activities, or who needed to be available to take care of Paul's aging parents.

Cheryl was married to Paul's brother, Alan, and if I were to describe her, I would say she was 'the calm in the storm.' She was the coordinator of most Withey activities and the go-to person when logic needed to prevail.

As for Roland, if you didn't know him and ran into him on the street, very likely you would be intimidated by his size. His six-foot four-inch frame and broad shoulders quickly overshadowed anyone and everything in his surroundings. But every family needs a teddy bear, and Roland was just that for the Withey clan. Two minutes after being introduced to him, everyone knew that his heart was as big as he was. He was tough when he needed to be and protective to a fault, but Amanda was his Achilles heel. She could reduce him to a puddle with just one smile.

When they arrived at my door, I showed them to the rooms I had set up for each of them. After they put their things away and unpacked the clothes they would be wearing to the funeral the next day, we gathered in the family room to catch up.

Roland, being the consummate gentleman, immediately said, "Thank you so much for letting us stay with you."

"It is truly my pleasure. I know you both realize how much this means to Jennifer and Paul that you are here representing the family from Canada. Honestly, we welcome all the love and support we can get right now. This has been a really long week for us. I never thought when I woke up on Monday morning that I would be burying my granddaughter on Friday."

I grabbed a tissue from the side table and wiped away another set of tears. I kept thinking there were none left in me, but obviously, there were still more tears to be shed.

"I know what you mean," said Roland. "This is not what I thought I would have been doing either."

"Funerals are not anyone's favorite things," Cheryl said, doing her best to hold back the tears.

"But it is an honor to be here for the rest of the family. They would have all wanted to come if they could."

"Jennifer and Paul understand. They so appreciate that the two of you are here. Can I get you something to drink?"

"That would be nice. It's been a long day and a cup of tea would be lovely if you have any," said Cheryl.

"I'll take a Coke, if you have one," Roland chimed in.

I got them their drinks and sat on the hearth of the fireplace. All of us seemed to be deep in the same thought. How could this be happening?

Roland finally broke the silence. "As my family has so often accused me of, I tend to have a bit of a white-knight complex. Victims tend to evoke a lot of sympathy within me. That being said, Amanda was kind of *My Perfect Storm*. She was a beautiful spirit, with a lot going on inside, but only a little tiny trickle of it reaches out.

"I remember thinking the first time I met Amanda—this girl likes me. I wanted to believe that her glances and smiles were meant for me specifically, but realized they most likely were autonomic responses. I was a little sad at that thought because I really wanted her to like me." A smile crept across his face remembering that first meeting.

"That is so true. And with Amanda, it was really hard at first to know what she was trying to communicate to us," Cheryl added.

Roland was nodding his head in agreement. In the beginning none of us knew for certain

Amanda's thoughts, but as the years passed, it became very clear to anyone who was around her that you knew exactly what she was thinking.

Roland continued, "In the beginning, I let her restrictions cloud my understanding of her abilities. But with each visit, it was harder and harder to deny that there was much more going on than the outward appearance that we all saw.

"I wish I could remember that first conversation that made me realize that *My Girl* was having some pretty heavy cogitations. *My Sparkle* was nobody's vegetable. It was then that she became less of a pity case for me and more of a little buddy."

He stopped to reflect on the thought that was crossing his mind about what he had said.

"Amanda would have hated it if she ever thought she was a pity case. She was tiny, the wrong size and weight for a girl her age for the majority of her life. But Amanda was as straightforward as they come. It was easy to know what struck her fancy. And she had no qualms about expressing her displeasure when it concerned her." He laughed, clearly remembering one of those times.

"I don't think most people would be able to understand this, and I guess they could say my conversations with Amanda are subject to interpretation, or maybe validation that I belong on the funny farm. Others might only see a glance, or a tear, or a wince if she were in pain, and might think her communication was nonexistent."

But I knew exactly what he meant when he said, "I think she relied on us to supply the dialogue. And supply I did.... A conversation with her usually became more about me, her pain kind of layered on top of mine, her concerns my concerns. She was okay with that."

His words were validation for what I had felt for years. Conversations with Amanda were not what anyone would consider normal. His words were music to my ears. It validated again that so many of us had been having these unspoken conversations with Amanda all these years.

It may have been the long day of travel combined with the daunting task of the funeral that lay ahead of us, but for a moment, I don't think Roland wanted to continue our talk. The sadness of losing Amanda overwhelmed him again.

But then, as another memory came into focus, the smile returned to his eyes. "I think what stands out for me and what I wish the whole world could know about Amanda is that the lack of physicality had stolen her muscle tone, but it took none of her strength. She was without a doubt the strongest person I ever knew."

He had nothing left to say. The reality of the day had finally overwhelmed all of us. "Hope you are okay with me turning in. I want to put the finishing touches on my speech for tomorrow," he said as he rose from his chair.

There were tears in his eyes as he walked away, saying, "Damn, I'm going to miss that beautiful little girl."

Chapter 28

As we started preparing for the funeral that Friday morning, my emotions were vacillating between resentment and anger.

I resented that the sun was shining, that the blue sky was filled with wispy white clouds, no wind, and the temperature was hovering around 60 degrees. From a weather perspective, the day was perfect.

I was angry because I couldn't comprehend how it could be so flawless. The sadness of the day was overwhelming and I felt that the weather should be just as gloomy as we all were.

I was angry that I had to watch my daughter bury her child. We all knew from the start that Amanda wasn't going to be in our lives forever. But when the reality slaps you in the face, you wish you had a punching bag to hit.

But then I realized Amanda wasn't going to allow her last life event to be marred with rain, lightning, or freezing cold temperatures. She wanted everyone to see how glorious a planet we live on. She wanted family and friends to come together and talk about how spectacular the day was in every way.

As the time for the service drew close, I was amazed to see the number of people who had shown up to support the family. The chapel was overflowing with flowers and plants. Every available seat was filled. People were lined up on the sides of the room as well as sitting in the vestibule leading into the chapel.

Similar to a wedding, there is usually an order to the start of a memorial service. Amanda's service followed that protocol of having the family along with the pallbearers walking in right before the service started.

However, there was one small difference. As I had mentioned before, a big part of Amanda's life was cheering her brother and his teammates through many baseball games. And it wasn't just in the spring. Baseball in Texas is year-round.

Two days before the funeral Justin approached his Mom with an idea. He and his teammates wanted permission to come to the funeral in their baseball uniforms. If you are a stickler for protocol, it's possible that the idea of seeing kids at a funeral in baseball uniforms could offend you. But Amanda had been their designated mascot for years, and it was their way of honoring her.

I had been emotional all day, but seeing those boys walk in together, their hats over their hearts, was a statement like none I had ever seen at a funeral. Those boys were honoring her with their show of solidarity. She was used to seeing them in uniform and that was how they wanted her to remember them.

Chapter 29

The services began once the team was seated. Coach Andy had agreed to officiate. "Thank you all for being here. Jennifer, Paul, and the rest of the family want you to know how much it means to them that you are here to celebrate Amanda's life.

"She was a beautiful soul who touched the lives of many although she never said a word. Her gift to the world was her smile which she gave without hesitation to everyone she came in contact with. It was the one thing I could always count on every time this group of boys sitting here today as a team took the field, Amanda would be there with a smile. We are all going to miss that smile."

He led the participants in a quick prayer and then read the passage from the Bible which her parents requested—Romans 5:1-5. He talked about its meaning—how suffering produces perseverance; perseverance, character; and character, hope. Amanda had no doubt suffered, but she took that suffering and turned it into hope for many.

Next on the agenda, were words from Roland, Paul and myself. Most everyone knew the majority of the people who were there, but few except family knew the man who was first to walk up to the podium.

Roland explained that he was given the honor of speaking for the Canadian contingent that was back home wishing they were there to celebrate Amanda's life. He apologized for not being able to speak off the cuff. Said it would just be too difficult. He explained that he had written something that he wanted to share with those in attendance, so he would be reading from his copy.

It might have seemed odd, but the room full of Texans immediately embraced the words of the Canadian giant that was standing in front of them. Houston is not a hockey town, but anytime you use sports as an analogy—regardless of the sport—the folks in the room will get it.

His voice was as big as he was as he read the speech he had written.

"One could assume upon seeing me from a distance, that I was perhaps an aging, knuckle-dragging enforcer from some minor league hockey farm team. While sadly devoid of any actual athletic talent, I do identify with this model.

I think (in my buried subconscious) that I am the defense for team Withey. Goon to the stars of our team: the sons, daughters, nieces, nephews, and assorted cousins in our extended clan. In my idiot brain, I am the rabid wolf, chained to the gate. Defender of all things sweet, innocent, and uncorrupted.

It is for this reason that Amanda is the perfect instrument of my undoing—My Kryptonite. All this because you see, Amanda used to be the star center on another team. The center of a different universe.

While in her freshman season with that team there was a terrible locker room incident. Because of her injuries, after this, she needed to change teams. She came to our team already on the injured list. Perhaps she would never play again. Fortunately, for team Withey, Coaches Jennifer and Paul have an eye for talent.

Her status put me in a quandary. How do you protect someone who is already injured? How do you guard someone who already has a crack defense set up? Simple. Change roles. Despite limited ice time, I resolved to become love incarnate.

Tired hockey analogies aside, I decided to be 'THAT UNCLE.' Every time I saw her face, I sang 'Amanda, light of my life. He could have made you a gentleman's wife.'

When it didn't cause her stress, I would carry her (the lightest of possible burdens) and when that became too much, we just held hands.

"Oh good," I thought, "She likes me," as her grin lit up. I never realized how much our spread-out visits meant to her until I came for a summer visit.

We drove in to Houston and came to the house. Hugs and kisses were distributed, and I broke off to pay my respects to 'Mi'Lady' and King Rod. 'Oh look Amanda! Uncle Roland's here!'

Wham! The lights come on and it's game time. My heart leaped. I laid a hug and kiss on Rodney. That was cool 'cause we're bros.

I made my way over to Amanda. Now I know where they keep the Northern Lights in summer. Those eyes were flashing! I sang my silly song, planted a kiss, and we held hands for a while as I talked about my trip.

After about ten minutes, I made as if to go and rejoin the group. A slow low sigh. A single tear tracked from her right eye to the ridge of her jaw. Well. I'm done.

If you want, you can tell me how Amanda's condition sometimes results in involuntary spasms and random noises. How it's natural, but does not mean anything.

You could. If you want to walk upright in the future, sporting all your teeth? Perhaps it might be best you didn't.

I don't care how big and bad you are. When a little kid hands you a toy phone, you answer it. When a little girl wants you to play 'Tea Party' you become 'Mrs. Nesbitt.' When a beautiful young woman asks you to stay just a little longer, you sit your ass down and stay a little longer.

It was my last, best, half hour with star forward Amanda Withey as she drifted off to a nap. I should have known better. Stayed longer.

Ladies and Gents, it's a proud moment for the home team. One of our star players, career All-Star, power forward, and team captain, Amanda

Withey has been traded to the Majors. My girl is in the big show, on God's team 'Heavens Angels.'

Good job, Coach."

• • •

Funerals are a funny thing. We all walk through the door braced for the seriousness of the occasion, but when people start reminiscing, both laughter and tears result. Roland's words brought both to the crowd.

The light that Amanda brought to everyone's life was unmistakable. Unfortunately, no matter how much we all tried to forget, the one thought that was always in the back of all of our minds was how she ended up on the injured reserve list that Roland mentioned.

It was obvious to even a blind person the love Roland had for Amanda. Thoughts of her brought smiles to his eyes, but the pain in his heart that day came through with his every word. What wasn't written on the copy of the speech that Roland gave was what he said at the very end. He started to walk away, but then hesitated. For the first time, his anger about Amanda's condition could no longer be contained.

He raised his eyes to the heavens and said what I had wanted to say for years.

"God says we have to forgive, and I will do my best to follow His words and Amanda's example. But God help the person who did this to her. They better hope we never cross paths."

Many were perplexed by what he said. Only close family and friends knew how Amanda ended up in the condition in which we got her. I, along with the rest of the family, knew what he meant. Not sure if there was anyone who knew Amanda's story that didn't have that very same thought cross their minds at some point.

But the gentle giant, our team's enforcer, as much as he might want to, would never allow himself to hurt another human being, no matter how much they deserved it. He would think about it. He would wish he could, but in the end, he would know that it wouldn't be what Amanda would want. He would leave that job to the Big Guy upstairs.

Chapter 30

As Roland stepped away from the podium, it was the moment I had looked forward to and dreaded. Half of me was filled with the fear that I would break down crying uncontrollably. The other half wanted everyone to know what a remarkable life Amanda had lived.

Unlike Roland, I hadn't been smart enough to write down everything I was going to say. I had Paul Bohman's letter to Amanda from her Sweet Sixteen party, but for the most part I was taking a page from Zack's playbook from her birthday party—I was just going to wing it.

"This is harder than I thought it was going to be," I admitted to the crowd, dabbing a tear off my cheek.

"Sorry, everyone. This is the day I've been dreading ever since I met Amanda. I knew it would happen eventually, but after years of her defying the odds over and over again, I think I was lulled into a false sense of security."

I stopped to catch my breath. I was trying to collect my thoughts when Amanda's voice flittered across my brain.

"It's Okay, Granny. Just say what's in your heart and everything will be okay."

That thought reminded me how much she enjoyed being there for someone else.

"I'm sure some of you are confused by my appearance. I know it is customary to wear black at a funeral, but as you can see most of the family has on red. It was Amanda's favorite color. So it is in honor of her that we come together dressed in the color that would make her smile.

"I know it may sound hard to believe, but almost nine years ago, part of me already knew exactly what I would share at her funeral. Just didn't think it would be so soon.

"The sentiments in an email that Paul Bohman sent to be read at Amanda's sixteenth birthday party have never been far from my thoughts. He spoke of seeing her running through fields chasing, butterflies, of sneaking her first kiss, of getting into trouble, and blaming her brothers. He wrote about how she was writing a novel deep within her mind. How she would fill it with imagination and love, and how we would someday laugh and cry as we all read it together."

I was wishing I had a glass of water because my throat was so dry. It seemed the amount of tears I had cried had finally taken their toll and dehydrated my body.

"It may seem ironic, but one of the last conversations I had with Amanda was right before Christmas. I told her I was going to turn her life into a book. That I was going to give her the voice she never had.

"She was happier than I had ever seen her. The thought of the world knowing all the good she had accomplished filled her with pride."

I turned to the casket and said, "My sweet girl, I promise I will finish the story that I've started. I will tell the world what you have done and how privileged we have all been to have shared these past twenty years with you.

"I love you, Manda Panda."

I walked back to my seat with tears rolling down my face. My Uncle Bill put his arm around me and gave me a kiss on the cheek as he whispered, "You did good. Amanda would be proud."

I wanted to let the floodgates of my feelings out, but instead just laid my head on his shoulder.

Chapter 31

Paul was last in our series of tributes. He, like Roland, had been smart enough to write down what he wanted to say.

"Thank you all for being here as we celebrate the life of Amanda. Not sure if everyone knows this, but the name Amanda means *worthy of love*."

"How appropriate. Not necessarily the love we all gave to her, but the love she gave to us.

"I could go through the times of her life that I remember so vividly. Like when we first got her—we were sold on her before we even met her in person. How I was privileged to watch her eyes come into focus. The times I played 'find my eyes' with her and clapped her hands.

"Amanda saw more than most people because we took her everywhere—Blackwater Falls, Yellowstone, Mt. Rushmore, Banff, and many trips to Texas and Arkansas.

"She went to church, t-ball games, soccer games, baseball games, basketball games, hockey games, softball games, even more baseball games."

Everyone laughed.

"I remember holding her left hand to calm her down. Giving her Eskimo kisses. Watch her cheer when the Steelers made a good play rather than the Cowboys in Super Bowl XXX."

Again another laugh from the crowd.

"But the biggest thing we will all remember Amanda for is her smile." His face was grinning from ear to ear.

"Her smile — It was contagious. You couldn't help, but smile back. It made us feel so good.

"She watched her brothers, sister, and cousins grow up and loved to smile at them. She gave a smile to everyone."

He stopped and looked over at her in her casket—smiling because he knew Amanda was at peace.

"But what was so different about her smile was that it was so meaningful. That smile even got her several bridesmaid jobs."

He was gazing into the sea of faces in the chapel as he said, "And I'm sure that each and every one of you has a story about sometime you met or saw Amanda and it probably involved her smile."

He was a proud dad as he said, "I want every person here to remember something. If Amanda was able to have this kind of positive impact on the world without being able to walk or talk, then look at the impact each of us could have on the people we're around every day—if we only smile."

He stopped briefly as his words resonated with the crowd. "To me, this is Amanda's message to the world:

Love God
Love People
Smile

"Thank you so much for sharing this day with us. Please join us for the conclusion of the services in the cemetery. Also know that our friends at Calvary Chapel are providing a meal for everyone, so I hope you will join us."

• • •

The services at the gravesite were more difficult than I thought they would be. The baseball team was standing together by the fence to the left hand side of the plot. Justin, Katie, and Caden stood at the foot of the casket, arms linked together. Jennifer and Paul were sitting facing Amanda's casket and holding onto Joseph and Adison as tightly as they could without cutting off circulation. Marcia, Geri, and I, along with Iris and my Uncle Bill were sitting behind them.

Right before they were going to lower Amanda into the ground, Jennifer got up and took roses out of the spray that was covering the casket and handed them to us and several others.

Not something I had done before at a funeral, but we stayed until after the maintenance crew had moved the concrete cover over the vault and filled the hole with dirt and covered it with sod.

We had stayed as long as we could. It was time to go have dinner and share stories about Amanda with our loved ones and friends one more time.

Reality would soon dictate that we had to get back to our jobs. To go about living life the best way we could without the smile that we had all become so accustomed to.

• • •

A couple of weeks after Amanda's funeral, there was one more reminder of the effect she had on others. Justin was playing a game at Lutheran South Academy. This school had graciously allowed this homeschool team to use their baseball diamond as their home field for several years.

Prior to the start of the game, as both teams were lined up on their respective baselines, Justin was called to home plate.

The LSA team had something they wanted to give to Justin and his family.

This group of teenagers had gotten together and had a plaque designed for the family. The inscription on the top portion read:

In Memory of Amanda Withey

With Love from Lutheran South Academy

•••

"But those who trust in the Lord will find strength

They will soar high on wings like eagles"

Isaiah 40:31

The bottom half had a copy of the picture from Jennifer's Facebook page of Amanda holding Justin's game ball. On the other side was a metal holder that held a ball with signatures from every member of the LSA baseball team.

Chapter 32

They say the first year after someone dies is the hardest. It's the first family gatherings, the first birthday parties, and the celebration of the various holidays. The one that everyone says is the worst however, is that first Christmas.

We made it through Thanksgiving, but Black Friday shopping wasn't the same as before. It amazed me how many things I passed thinking, *Amanda would really like this.*

Getting ready for Christmas opened a completely new set of feelings. Something was just off and it was hard to get into the spirit, as they say. But then as always, Amanda brought a new wonder to our world.

Jennifer called and asked me to come to the house. She had something to show me.

When I walked in, the smiles that greeted me were bigger than normal. After I got hugs from everyone, Jennifer began to tell me the story of the newest addition to their Christmas tradition.

"You know, Mom, the last two days have been harder than most. Decorating for the holidays has brought the pain of losing Amanda to the forefront on all of our minds." I could see the tears forming, and although they were sad, there were tears of joy mixed in as well.

"I know Marcia and I give you a hard time about some of the things you have done for the kids. You do have a tendency to spoil them. I have to admit, there were times when I questioned what my five kids were going to do with the ornaments you gave them each year. I sometimes felt it was a little over the top. And I often wondered what Amanda would ever do with all those ornaments."

She paused and took a deep breath. I was seeing that look that I had seen so many times over the past few months. Each of us has some form of being empathic, whether it is wincing when we see someone fall and skin their knee or cringing when someone gets their fingers slammed in a door. I had come to see the tells in Jennifer's face and body language.

I could feel the lump in my throat mimicking the one I knew was coming up in hers. I could feel my eyes water as I saw the tears in her eyes. I could feel the goosebumps forming on my arms as I watched her try and regain her composure.

She continued, "You know, Mom, it wasn't until yesterday, that we all realized those ornaments weren't really for Amanda. Instead, they were for us. Amanda loved it each year as we put her angels on the tree. She was always so excited when she opened the Hallmark box with the next angel you would give her." The tears were rolling down her face now, but the smile was reminiscent of the one I had cherished when I was talking with Amanda.

"Look what your grandkids, Paul, and I did last night."

There in the corner was the most beautiful six-foot-tall, pencil-thin tree covered with white lights. It was adorned with red bows, some solid, while others had white lettering that spelled out Peace, Joy, Happy Holidays, or Season's Greetings.

It was topped with a solid red star. But the jewels were the twenty angel ornaments I had given Amanda over the years. I couldn't hold back my tears any longer. I was completely overwhelmed with seeing the smiles on my grandkids' faces.

I have to admit, with seven grandkids and close to one hundred ornaments bought over time, I certainly don't remember all of them. But as I examined each of the angels, I was reminded of the smile on Amanda's face each time we took a new one out of its box for her.

"Granny, look at this," Adison said, pointing to the angel at the top of the tree. "It's the very first angel you gave Amanda."

As I held it in my hand, I marveled at the beauty of that first ornament. It was a gorgeous blue angel that appeared to be the same age that Amanda was when I gave it to her in 1995. This little cherub was sitting on a cloud holding a star.

"This one is my favorite. It's the one you gave her last year," said Joseph.

That angel was very different from all the others. It wasn't the normal image of an angel, but instead was an angel, cast as a bell and it played a song.

"Mom, I can't believe how much joy this tree with these keepsakes has brought to our family,"

Jennifer said. "The fact that the last one is a bell reminds me of the scene from the movie *It's a Wonderful Life*."

I knew exactly what she was talking about. It was when Clarence told George, "Every time you hear a bell ring, it means that some angel's just got their wings."

Our angel now had her wings.

I could feel Amanda looking down on us, so pleased with how she could still affect lives without ever saying a word. She loved smiling at others, but her reward was seeing smiles on people's faces. It was the smiles looking back at me that told me everything was going to be all right.

Chapter 33

A few weeks after Amanda's tree had been put up, the family gathered at my house for Christmas dinner. We laughed and enjoyed the day, but the void in the room could not be denied.

I watched as each grandchild opened their ornament of the year. I was momentarily filled with sadness because there was no new angel for Amanda. Watching the smile that came across her face every time she saw the latest angel always filled my heart with joy.

After the big presents, the tradition of the stocking bags marked the ending of our day. Fifteen years earlier, we had decorated large canvas bags because the amount of 'stuff' that I would get for everyone would no longer fit in the stockings that decorated the mantel.

It was my favorite gift to the kids and the one part of the day they looked forward to the most. The bags were a treasure trove of items to be used throughout the year. They might hold a favorite new video game or movie, gift cards to a favorite food place, Christmas scratch offs, candy, pens, and sticky notes. Everything carefully bought to remind them that they had a granny who was thinking of them.

As I had done every year, the gift bags were spread across my bed ready for me to fill. I had put Amanda's stocking on the nightstand. Like most things I had for Amanda, it was adorned with an angel drawn in silver glitter puff paint. But this year, Amanda's stocking bag would be empty and my heart was heavy with that thought.

The distribution of the stockings was the icing on the cake so to speak. I was relieved that we had made it through the day without breaking down in tears as a group. But my sweet daughter had other ideas and had one last gift for the family.

"Okay, everyone. I have something I need to share," Jennifer said.

The room went quiet which isn't easy with twenty-one people crowded into the living room.

As she stood in front of all of us, Jennifer took a deep breath, "I promised myself I wasn't going to cry. So much for following through with that idea."

She continued, as she wiped away a tear. "As all of you know, to say that Amanda's death has been hard on me is an understatement. There were days when the pain of missing Amanda was crushing. It would have been so easy to give into depression, but these four sweet faces that are staring at me and wondering what I'm about to say, had to come first. Collapsing into the despair I felt at times wasn't an option.

"This year has been transforming in more ways than one. And just like my mom," she said, looking at me and rolling her eyes, "I'm not real good with letting others know how I'm feeling or when I need help. I'm tough, and I'm supposed to be able to handle everything."

At that moment, I was feeling a little guilty for always hiding behind the tough façade that I presented to the world, even when I felt I was going to fall apart.

Each of us deals with death in our own way and for Jennifer, instead of reaching out to a therapist she found her answer with a nutritional specialist. He was the husband of a fellow Classical Conversations mom. Other friends had seen him to help with their health and personal issues and had achieved incredible results, so Jennifer decided it couldn't hurt to see if he could help with the sadness that she felt.

"When I first went to see Aaron, I didn't know what to expect. I've never been one to want to take any medication—wonder where I get that from?"

She smiled at me as she said that. Then she grinned and said, "Apple? Tree?"

I laughed. Guilty as charged.

She said, "I was looking for anything that would help me stay focused. One of the first things Aaron told me was to start keeping a food log. What I didn't realize was that the app on my phone would keep reminding me that I needed to walk ten thousand steps every day as well. I wasn't even coming close. So I adjusted the settings and made a goal of doing five thousand. That didn't work either.

"I don't know what made me do it, but as I started to feel better physically as I was eating better, I felt I needed to walk. I felt Amanda was telling me that I needed to see the world from a different perspective. That she was whispering in my ear that walking would show me things about the world that I never realized. Honestly, I was just hoping I would find some peace and serenity in those walks.

"In the beginning, I have to admit that I walked mindlessly, meandering through the subdivision. I didn't think of anything other than making the goal and eventually, I worked my way up to consistently walking ten thousand steps a day. But after a couple of weeks, I started to notice how beautiful the world was when it started waking up. Flowers were covered with the morning dew. Ladybugs and bees were starting their daily journey to pollenate plants. Sometimes, I saw deer standing on the side of the road.

"When we were traveling, I was able to walk next to streams or around lakes. And for a few days when we were in Florida, I was able to listen to the sounds of the water lapping the shoreline."

It was amazing to watch the peace that had settled on Jennifer's face. Those walks had taught her not just about the beauty of this big blue marble we call home, but about the meditative benefits of being at one with the world.

"When the beauty was too much to handle, I did what everyone eventually does. I started capturing what I saw with the camera on my phone. Whether it was the red, yellow, and purple skies of the sunrise, or the fog-covered roads where I could barely see five feet in front of me, there was a beauty that I had failed to appreciate before," Jennifer told us.

"In the beginning, I wasn't sure how I could share what I was seeing as well as feeling. But then I remembered how easy it was to put together the memories of our previous trips with Shutterfly. So I have put together a book of the snapshots I've taken over the last nine months. I have one for each family. I hope they mean as much to you as they have meant to me."

As Jennifer handed out the books, we all sat mesmerized by the pictures and the stories they told. The cover was a picture of a statue that looks to be a sweet little angel about four years old—the same age Amanda was when she and Paul brought her into their home. This sweet little angel figurine had short, wavy hair—the same length that Amanda's was when they first got her. She was dressed in a romper with a bit of a ruffle at the bottom, an outfit not unlike one of the first ones I saw Amanda in twenty years earlier at our first meeting. She was sitting with her legs bent and her head resting on her knees. Her eyes were closed, but the smile that adorned her face was reminiscent of Amanda's.

As I opened the book, and read the first page, the pictures and words overwhelmed my senses. The first image was of a tree, roots exposed, demonstrating the lengths it went to for survival. Jennifer's first words in the book were, "When our faith is tested, we find out how deep our roots are...."

Her faith had been tested many times during this journey, but she and Paul did their best to give Amanda a "normal" life. Their struggles with the education system were never ending. The battles with Medicaid and doctors were constant. Their fight for funds for respite care was often lost. But none of those struggles were as challenging as the one they faced with losing Amanda.

Even so, the book was a testament to the power of faith. It was a reminder that if we stop, look, and listen, we will see the beauty in life even when we don't want to.

Jennifer had written a note in the back of the book that she gave to me that I will always cherish.

Mom, We all knew that Amanda would not live forever, but her love of life made it impossible to imagine that we would actually ever lose her.

Thank you for always teaching me to reach out to others in love. We could have chosen not to love this little one and we would not be experiencing this loss, but we would not have experienced life to the fullest without her.

I knew I had made mistakes as a parent—who among us hasn't? But Jennifer's words reinforced what I knew in my soul, that my daughters were extraordinary people, and I was so very grateful to not only call them my daughters, but my friends as well.

Chapter 34

I have to admit, when I told Amanda I was going to turn her life into a book, her death was not the ending that I saw in my mind.

I assumed she would be the center of attention at the book launch. I saw her accompanying me to book signings. I expected she would be by my side as I spoke at events regarding people with special needs and how remarkable their lives are. I imagined the nodding of heads as I spoke about how what so many first see as a burden is somehow turned into a blessing.

I am at a loss as to how to end the tale of this beautiful young woman, because all I want to do is be able to turn back the clock. To somehow be transported back to 1994 so that I can tell Amanda's biological mother to not leave her baby that awful night. To warn her that she is about to lose the most precious gift that she will ever be given.

The feelings that course through my body are mixed. There is a part of me that is sad. If it wasn't for the brutality of that one night, Amanda might have been finishing college or holding her firstborn child instead of passing away at such a young age.

I feel sad that she never got to have the life that others had. Sad for those of us who are left behind who never again get to see her eyes dancing with delight as she watches the world move around her.

Proud of my daughter and son-in-law for the sacrifices they made to give Amanda as normal a life as they possibly could. Proud of her siblings, aunts, uncles, cousins, and friends who never once saw Amanda as being anything other than whole.

I'm happy for all the conversations we had and the memories of holidays, birthdays, and family events that we shared. I'm comforted by the thought of her beautiful eyes that reflected the depth of her soul. Those eyes will always be my *Love Blue*.

I'm honored to have been called her Granny for all those years. To have witnessed how unselfishly she gave of herself. Thankful for being shown that we should never take anything for granted. But more importantly, how precious this gift of life is. Amanda, through her smile, let each of us know that she cherished every minute of her existence.

I'm moved by the knowledge that even with all her limitations, Amanda was able to have such a positive impact on so many. That she was able to touch others without ever saying a word.

When I think of Amanda's life, what she accomplished and how she changed so many people, I can't help but be amazed. She taught us to seek the best out of every day that we are given on this beautiful planet we call earth.

She showed us that we each have our own destiny. That it is up to us as to whether we collapse into our own misery or make the most out of the cards that are dealt to us.

As a family, we move on without her, but we will never forget the beauty she brought to our lives. She may no longer be here, but her spirit continues to grace us as her influence changed us all. She showed us what could be accomplished with strength and determination.

Our final tributes to her as a family are the words that we had etched on her tombstone:

EYES THAT SPOKE

A SMILE THAT INSPIRED

Acknowledgements

As I stated in the prologue, I told Amanda that I would write her story and give her a voice. I did my best to capture her emotions and feelings in a way that would make her proud.

This story could not have been written without the support of so many people. However, it's the speech at the awards ceremony where you hope you don't forget someone.

Jennifer and Paul – They say the apple doesn't fall far from the tree, and I have no doubt that Amanda's gift was nurtured by what she received from the two of you. As do most children, they pattern themselves after the examples they get from their parents. Amanda gave of herself so completely, because that is what she learned from the two of you.

Marcia, Justin, Rodney, Caden, Bryce, Joseph, and Adison – As Amanda's aunt, siblings, and cousins, you loved her and embraced her just as she was. Your love for her never ceased to amaze me. It is a testament to the power of accepting others just as they are.

Bill Thurman and Paula Hinzman – You were Amanda's champions after that fateful night in October 1994. She was never able to say "Thank You" for all you did, so I'm saying it for her. The outcome of the trial wasn't what any of us wanted, but after the verdicts were rendered, she moved on and never looked back. She trusted that someday justice will prevail.

Paul B – It was your words that planted the seed in my brain about writing this book for Amanda and giving her a voice. I hope that I captured her spirit in a way that fulfilled the vision of the novel you saw her writing in her mind.

Mavis and Roland – When I reached out, you both gave me a piece of Amanda's story that touched my heart. The insights regarding your interactions with Amanda were perfect in helping show the effect she had on others.

To my friends/editors – Nora, Christy, Beth, and Reid. Every author needs people who will tell them the truth if the flow and transitions aren't right. Thank you all for reading and re-reading my manuscript countless times until it was worthy of Amanda's story.

To Cindy – Once again your magic has put my words onto pages and turned them into the fulfillment of my dream and promise to Amanda. Thank you from the bottom of my heart.

To the respite workers – Michelle, Amy, Alecia, Blair, Jackie, Shante, Ila and others – who helped care for Amanda over the years. She loved each of you and enjoyed the time you spent with her. You came into her life because it was a job, but left as friends.

James Bonnet – Thank you for teaching me the art of story. I learned so much as we talked through the elements of Amanda's story. You showed me how to stay focused and true to both Amanda and myself.

Bobby Schindler – Thank you for your insights into the chapter about your sister. They completed the vision of why Jennifer, Paul, and Amanda made the trip to Florida to support your family.

To everyone who reads this book – Thank you for taking the time to learn about a fearless young woman who did everything she could to be there for others. It is my hope that you share her story with family and friends. Her accomplishments and legacy lives on through each of you.

Made in the USA
Middletown, DE
21 February 2021

34135031R00126